Grace, Faith, Works
How Do They Relate?

Annual Preachers' Forum 1992

Harding University
Graduate School of Religion

Edited by Dr. C. Philip Slate

Publishing Designs, Inc.
Huntsville, Alabama 35810

Publishing Designs, Inc.
P. O. Box 3241
Huntsville, Alabama 35810

© 1992 by Harding University Graduate School
of Religion

Printed in the United States of America

ISBN 0-929540-14-X

Contents

Schedule
April 14, 1992

8:15 - 8:30   Welcome and Prayer

8:30 - 9:15   "An Historical-Theological Overview of the Grace-Works Issue" — John Mark Hicks (Memphis, Tenn.)

9:20 - 10:30   "Grace and Works in Ephesians 2:1-10 and Titus 2:11-14" — Richard Oster (Memphis, Tenn.) and William Woodson (Nashville, Tenn.)

10:30 - 10:45   Break

10:45 - 11:45   Small group discussion of first three presentations

11:45 - 1:00   Lunch (Alumnus of the Year Award, Citations)

1:00 - 2:10   "Grace and Works in Romans 4-5 and James 2:14-26" — Rubel Shelly (Nashville, Tenn.) and Keith Mosher (Memphis, Tenn.)

2:15 - 3:15   Small group discussion of the two 1:00 p.m. presentations

3:15 - 3:30   Break

3:30 - 4:45   Questions to the panel of five speakers

4:45 - 5:00   Prayer and conclusion

Introduction

The Forum, of which this book is a lightly edited transcript, occurred on April 14, 1992, in Memphis, Tennessee. The seven hundred or so people who came for the afternoon session forced us to move to the nearby White Station church building for more seating space. Except for that midday move, the proceedings took place as planned. It is hoped the resulting information will prove to be useful to all who read it.

These Forums are arranged by the Alumni Association officers of Harding University's Graduate School of Religion. All of them are graduates and involved in ministry of one type or another (Eddie Miller, President; and Bill Pratt, Roger Johnson, and Tom Steed, Vice-Presidents). Bill Flatt and I have worked with them on this project and enjoyed our association.

The annual intentions of the officers are to select some living and significant concern among Christians and then to chose competent people to discuss it for edification. Some topics become "hot" issues without being really significant, except for their potential to alienate people and trouble churches—like the number of cups on the Lord's table, women wearing pantsuits, and the like. Other topics are terribly important but rarely become "hot" issues—like evangelizing the idolatrous peoples of the world, alleviating the conditions of the destitute, and even personal holiness. But the topic for the Forum—the relationship between grace, faith, and works—is both significant and disputed, even "hot." Indeed, even in evangelical circles, it is a lively issue, even if some points of concern are different from the ones found here.

The format for the day was designed to enable people to hear carefully prepared presentations, to discuss them in small groups, and in those groups to generate significant questions to ask the speakers toward the end of the program. This is the third year to employ this format since people have responded favorably to the combination of speeches, group discussions, and focused questions. During the Question-Answer period, the questions came exclusively from the small group discussions rather than from the floor. In that period the panelists had opportunity to respond to each other for clarification and sharpening the focus.

While I am neither philosophically nor personally opposed to a debate format, that was not planned for April 14. Four of the speakers were scheduled in pairs to discuss the same texts, but they were never asked to respond to or debate each other. Rather, each one was asked to exegete the assigned texts and then draw out their legitimate implications for the way in which God's grace and the human response of faith and obedience are related. Four speakers knew what Dr. John Mark Hicks was going to say because he furnished each of them an early copy of his perspective/framework presentation on the background to the subject matter. But Dr. Hicks did not know what the others were going to say, and they did not know what each other would say. Obviously, each speaker knows much more than he had time to say. But the intention was for the five presentations combined to cover the major New Testament passages on the subject for the day.

I am grateful to Charles Patterson and Riverside Productions of Memphis for making the material available on audiocassette (order from Harding Bookstore, 1000 Cherry Road, Memphis, Tennessee 38117), and to James Andrews of Publishing Designs, Inc. of Huntsville, Alabama, for producing this printed version of the transactions. Except for endnote references to sources quoted and biblical references added to locate texts referred to orally, the printed version is only a lightly edited (by each speaker and myself) version of what was said. May God be glorified through both the thought and behavior resulting from this material.

C. Philip Slate, Editor

John Mark Hicks

John Mark Hicks is an Associate Professor of Christian Doctrine at Harding University Graduate School of Religion. He also serves as Adjunct Faculty at Christian Brothers University. He has served as Associate Professor of Bible and Ministry at Magnolia Bible College, Adjunct Faculty at Capstone School of Ministry in Tuscaloosa, Alabama, and as Assistant Professor of Theology at Southern Christian University. In 1981, he served as instructor at Northeastern Christian Junior College in Villanova, Pennsylvania. From 1979 to 1980, he was instructor at Potter Bible School in Bowling Green, Kentucky.

He received the A.A. and B.A. degrees from Freed-Hardeman University (1976, 1977), the M.A.R. from Westminster Theological Seminary (1979), the M.A. from Western Kentucky University, and the Ph.D. from Westminster Theological Seminary (1985).

John Mark and Barbara Adcox Hicks have three children: Ashley Dawn, Joshua Mark, and Rachel Nicole.

Articles have been published in *Restoration Quarterly*, *Evangelical Journal*, *Gospel Advocate*, *Firm Foundation*, *Sound Doctrine*, *Image*, *Mission*, and others. Of his four academic presentations, one was "The Righteousness of Saving Faith: Arminian versus Remonstrant Grace" (Arminius Convocation, Evangelical School of Theology, 1991).

John Mark holds membership in American Society of Church Historians, Sixteenth-Century Society, Evangelical Theological Society, Society of Christian Philosophers, and Evangelical Philosophical Society. Among his many honors, he has recently been selected for International Who's Who and Who's Who in Religion.

An Historical-Theological Overview of the Grace-Works Issue

John Mark Hicks

I appreciate the opportunity of being here. I will be participating with two former teachers, brother Woodson and brother Shelly, and two colleagues in this town, brother Mosher and brother Oster. I appreciate them all and I hope that our time together this morning and this afternoon will be of great benefit to all of us.

The pilgrim is an alien in search of a home. He is a stranger in a hostile country whose hope is to find rest. Peter uses this concept to describe the scattered Christians of Asia Minor. In 1 Peter 2:11 his readers are addressed as "strangers and pilgrims" or "aliens and exiles." Their search for a home, however, is not an uncertain one. The biblical concept of hope as expectation and anticipation is clearly articulated in 1 Peter 1:3-9. We as Christians have experienced a new birth which gives us a living hope. It is a hope grounded in the resurrection of Jesus and sustained by the power of God through faith. We wait for, anticipate, and expect the revelation of our hope in the last time. The pilgrim here is not an uncertain wanderer who is in doubt of his destiny or quaking in his boots about the prospect of what might or might not happen in the last time. Rather, he is certain of his salvation. He rejoices in his hope. Hope is what sustains the pilgrim in a hostile society.

In the history of theology, however, the concept of pilgrim underwent a significant development which reversed this biblical concept of hope. One of the best illustrations of this is the trial and execution of Joan of Arc in 1431. Her judges condemned her on the basis of this pronouncement (among others):

> This woman sins when she says she is as certain of being received into Paradise as if she were already of partaker of it . . . seeing that on this earthly journey no pilgrim knows if he is worthy of glory or of punishment, which the sovereign judge alone can tell.[1]

In medieval theology, the pilgrim was always "unworthy and uncertain of his homeland."[2]

This approach to hope, an uncertain wishful thinking, or an uncertain groping in the twilight, was a focal point of Roman Catholic theology in the sixteenth century. Even the pope himself could not be certain of his salvation, and anyone who claimed certainty regarding his or her eternal destiny was anathema. The medieval pilgrim is lost in a sea of uncertainty. His hope is a mixture of fear and doubt. He cannot *feel* certain about his eternal destiny.[3]

This is quite different from the biblical pilgrim who through faith is certain of his hope. The biblical pilgrim knows he has eternal life (1 Jno. 5:13). But why the change? Why the development from the certain hope pictured in scripture to an uncertain one in late medieval theology? The answer to that question lies in the larger issue of the relationship between grace and works.

The sixteenth century saw a widespread rebellion against the anxiety and uncertainty that late medieval piety created. While the Reformation had its intellectual and scholarly dimensions, the roots of this tremendous explosion of religious activity in the early sixteenth century are found in the release that people experienced from the burden of religion.[4] The Roman Catholic system of works, its system of penance and absolution, had become oppressive. It institutionalized guilt rather than freeing the believer from it.

The central concept of late medieval theology is that God made a covenant with man to accept as righteous something that is not truly righteous. God determined to accept man's best efforts as meritorious, even though they are not in themselves meritorious. While those efforts could never earn salvation on their own terms in the context of strict justice, God determined to accept something less than what strict justice demanded. Instead of perfect obedience by which genuine merit is earned, God would now accept something less on the part of man's obedience. He would ask man to measure up to something less than perfect righteousness, but measure up nonetheless.

However, this places a tremendous burden on human effort. While the standard is lower, we still must measure up to it. The key phrase that characterizes these attempts is that everyone must do his best. God will not deny grace to anyone who is doing his best.[5]

The problem, however, is that although we may be certain of God's mercy in granting his grace to those that do their best, no one is certain that he has, in fact, done his best. For example, in order to do your best, you must love God with all your heart. Yet we all recognize that even our best efforts are flawed. Since it is nearly impossible to be certain that we are doing our very best, we can never be sure that we are in a state of grace. This kind of assurance creates deep anxiety, doubt, and fear. Have I measured up? Do I feel sorry enough? Have I done enough? Do I love

God deeply enough? It was this kind of assurance that Luther found fundamentally unsatisfying and unbiblical.

In 1505, Luther became a monk in the wake of a terrifying encounter with possible death. He quickly found his life as a monk a terrifying experience as well. Through the rigor of the Augustinian Order, Luther came to believe that his soul felt and drank "nothing but eternal punishment."[6] Even though he was the best monk one could be,[7] Luther was plagued with doubt about his salvation and he feared God's judgment.

Luther's problem with assurance was that he viewed the righteousness of God as a punishing righteousness to which man must measure up. In order to be considered righteous in God's sight, one has to be genuinely righteous. He has to perform works of righteousness, that is, he has to do righteousness, to be righteous in order to achieve this standard of God's righteousness so as to avoid punishment. Consequently, assurance rests on one's assessment of his own righteousness: whether he has effectively measured up, whether he has been good enough.

Luther broke through this anxiety when he came to a new understanding of what the "righteousness of God" means in Romans. Previously he had understood that righteousness as solely the justice of by which he punishes sinners. Now he came to understand it as the righteousness which God gives to believers to believers in Christ. The righteousness of God is the right standing God gives to believers on the basis of the work of Christ. The righteousness of God is not something to be feared, but to be received in faith.

Luther distinguished between active righteousness and passive righteousness.[8] Active righteousness is one which we earn for ourselves. It is our personal righteousness. Passive righteousness is a righteousness which we receive but we did not earn or personally achieve. It is a righteousness that comes from outside of ourselves as opposed to one that comes from within us. It is the difference between saving ourselves by our own personal righteousness through measuring up or by being saved by God's gift of righteousness in Christ through faith.

This was a breakthrough of assurance for Luther. Instead of being the struggling sinner who was constantly in doubt of his salvation and living in fear of the punishing righteousness of God, he now became the confident believer who stands righteous in the sight of God on the basis of Christ's work. Instead of the believer who works to measure up to a standard of righteousness in order to be saved, he now became the assured believer who has accepted God's gift of righteousness in Christ. Instead of wondering whether he was righteous enough in the sight of God, he now knew that in Christ God counted him righteous despite his struggles with sin.

Luther's response to late medieval theology yielded two important theological distinction which I think are biblically rooted.

First, there is a distinction between the ground of our salvation and the means by which we appropriate it. The ground of our salvation is the merit by which we stand before God. It is that which earns our righteous standing before God. The means by which we are saved is the method of appropriation. It is the way in which we receive our righteous standing before God.

The ground of our salvation is wholly outside of ourselves. It is external to us; it come from outside of us. Titus 3:5 explicitly denies that we are saved by "works of righteousness," that is, works which earn righteousness. We are not saved on the basis of the merit of our obedience or works. We are not saved on the ground that we are good enough. Rather, we are saved by the merits of Christ and not our own. It is the righteousness of God that is imputed to us as a gift. The righteousness by which we are saved is not earned or churned up by our own moral and positive obedience. Our obedience, no matter how blameless it may be, will never be sufficient to earn us a righteous, perfect standing before God.

It is in this sense that we can say salvation is wholly of God, that is, the merit or righteousness by which we are justified in the sight of God is not our own; it is the gift of God. The ground of our salvation, then, is the grace of God alone as it is offered to us in Christ Jesus. We are justified on the merits of what Christ has done, not on the merits which we have earned. He imputes to us a righteousness which is not our own.

Salvation, however, does not come to everyone. This gift of righteousness is not universally distributed. Rather, it is given to believers. Without faith no one can please God or enter into his presence since it is through faith that God gives his gift of righteousness. Faith is the means by which we receive the righteousness that comes from God. As a means, it does not contribute to the merit of our righteous standing, but it is the instrument by which the righteousness from God is received. The gift is the righteousness; faith is the open hand that receives the gift. Faith is a human act which responds to God's gracious offer of the gift of righteousness by accepting it. Faith, then, as a human act, is the means or instrument by which we appropriate salvation.

The second point is that there is a distinction between justification where righteousness is imputed to us and sanctification where we grow in personal holiness before God. Justification is the act of God which is accounted to believers so that we stand before him as if we had never sinned. We are acquitted of our sins. We are declared righteous. We stand righteous before God because God has imputed to us a righteousness which we did not earn.

Sanctification, however, in its progressive sense, refers to the process by which we as Christians grow in personal holiness. In the context of progressive sanctification, we seek to be transformed by the renewing of our minds into the image of Christ (Rom. 12:1,2).[9]

Justification, then, is a forensic, legal declaration of righteousness. We are acquitted of any guilt before the judgment seat of Christ. We stand righteous in the sight of God on the ground of the work of Christ, and through faith in Christ's propitiation, we receive God's gift of righteousness. There are no degrees of righteousness here. Justification is the gift of God's righteousness which is one hundred percent and is in no way defective.

Sanctification, however, is a process of growth that does involve a matter of degrees. Some Christians are weak in faith, others are strong. Some are immature, others are mature. Some display more of the Spirit's fruit than others. Through faith, we grow in personal holiness, in personal righteousness. We seek to serve God and are devoted to good works. We improve our service, our moral behavior, and our brotherly relationships with each other through the process of that growth. We seek to be more and more conformed to the image of God's Son as we live our life in this present evil age.

Justification, then, is a forensic declaration in the great throne room of God's heavenly court by which we are accounted righteous in his sight. Sanctification is that process of faith by which we seek to conquer sin in our lives in this earthly pilgrimage. We are righteous in the sight of God and, at the same time, people who through weakness continue to sin even though we strive for holiness.

Luther correctly perceived the fundamental flaw in late medieval theology. Justification is not something we earn through our own personal holiness. Rather it is a standing we freely receive by faith; it is a gift of righteousness which

God bestows on us in Christ. The righteousness by which we are saved is not something that we have churned up for ourselves; it is not an inherent righteousness. While we are called to grow in holiness, this personal righteousness does not contribute to the merit of our standing before God or else we could boast in ourselves rather than Christ. If we contribute to the merit, then we can boast about our contribution. Justification and sanctification must be distinguished in order to preserve assurance and exclude boasting.

The two distinctions that I have just made raise some significant questions about assurance. What is the basis of my assurance if I am both righteous in the courtroom of God and sinner in my earthly existence? On the one hand, as I look at the sin in my life and the struggles of my own weaknesses, how can I be assured? On the other hand, if I am righteous in the sight of God, what does it matter that I sin? These questions get to the heart of the issue because they raise the question of the relationship between justification and sanctification.

There are two extremes which must be avoided as we attempt to answer this important question. The question—which I believe is the real issue in this discussion of grace and works—is, if grace saves through faith, that is, if I am justified by faith on the basis of a righteousness that is not my own, how progressive must my sanctification be in order to retain my standing before God?

One extreme is antinomianism. Progressive sanctification implies a submission to law. We are under the law of God as his creatures and we bear an inherent responsibility to obey it and serve God. We as Christians must fulfill the law of Christ, the law of liberty (Gal. 6:2; Jas. 2:12). When progressive sanctification is effectively severed and unrelated to justification, then antinomianism results. If progressive sanctification is disconnected from justification, then justification is secured irrespective of sanctification. Consequently, personal holiness and service before God bear no relation to salvation or justification. There is, then, no need to be concerned about obeying God's law. Antinomianism, in its rankest forms, means that no matter how I live my life, no matter how often I rebel against God, I remain justified by faith. This severs the sanctification of the believer from any meaningful relationship to his salvation.

In the history of theology, pure antinomianism is difficult to find.[10] Both Lutherans and Calvinists have had to deal with groups within their traditions which were antinomian in slant. Luther himself wrote a book entitled, *Against the Antinomians*.[11] Antinomianism appears in the context of those who stress "salvation by faith alone" to the extent that the necessity of sanctification and the works which exhibit it are denied. We find, for example, some hyper-Calvinists arguing that it does not matter if one is an adulterer or thief or murderer if he believes in Christ with some intellectual assent, then he can be assured of his salvation. The most extreme interpretations of the Calvinist doctrine of "once saved, always saved" end up in antinomianism. If I believed that I was elect, and that nothing I did, no sin I could commit—even a rebellious attitude—would undermine my justification, I would be an antinomian because sanctification would be totally severed from justification.

Our pioneer preachers rightly rejected such antinomianism as it was expressed in frontier Calvinism. The biblical picture is quite clear, and it is the attempt to interpret some of these passages by would-be antinomians that has made pure antinomianism so rare. Paul, for example, links sanctification (obedience to the law of God) to the day of judgment. We will be judged by the deeds done in the body (2 Cor. 5:10). God will reward each person according to his deeds (Rom. 2:6). The description of the great throne room scene in Revelation 20:12,13 relates the judgment of God to what good or evil the dead had done. In the context of these passages, antinomianism must be rejected. God has not completely severed justification from sanctification.

The other extreme is legalism. When progressive sanctification is too intimately tied to justification so that it becomes a further condition of justification, then progressive obedience to the law becomes the condition of salvation itself. Our salvation, then, depends on how well we keep the law. If our salvation depends on how well we keep the law, if it depends on our progressive sanctification, then the sixty-four thousand dollar question is: How progressive must our sanctification be in order to remain justified?

There is no suitable answer when the question is asked in this manner. Must I be fifty percent, sixty percent, or can I be ten percent on a scale of sanctification? Perhaps it is more complicated than that. Perhaps the percentage required of us is dependent not only on the amount of the law effectively kept, but also on how long we have been Christians. If you have been a Christian for only a year, then you are given a certain amount of "grace," or the benefit of the doubt. Perhaps if you have been a Christian for a year, ten percent is acceptable. But if you have been a Christian for twenty years, then your threshold level might be seventy percent.

The problem with this line of thought, of course, is that scripture gives us no such scale. Whatever the dividing line on that scale might be, it is something that none of us can decipher for ourselves, much less for others. Take, for example, the medieval criterion, "doing the best you can." None of us would deny that every Christian ought to do the best he can. But is any Christian really certain that he is doing the best he can, much less that another brother or sister is doing the best he or she can? In fact, our problem is that we often realize that we have not done the best we could. We all recognize that our level of progressive sanctification is deficient since it is not one hundred percent.

This view of salvation can never attain any assurance because it can never answer the fundamental question: How progressive must our sanctification be in order to remain justified? This approach to assurance burdens the believer with constant anxiety. It returns to the legalism of late medieval theology. It forces us to ask the questions, Have I been good enough? Have I done enough? Consequently, we can never feel saved because we are never sure that our level of sanctification is good enough. Deathbed assurance, then, becomes a conjectural recounting of the goodness of one's life rather than a trusting in God's gift of righteousness in Christ. To recount one's goodness as the basis of assurance is certainly to boast in works, a boasting that grace excludes. While our assurance is not based upon how or what we feel—on the contrary, it is based on God's promises to us in his inspired word—nevertheless, any system which does not permit a person to feel saved must be false.

How, then, are justification and sanctification related? If the two are not totally severed, but neither is justification dependent upon a certain level of sanctification, then what is it that relates these two aspects of our salvation? There is, I believe, a principle that links the two and unites them for our salvation. It is the principle of submissive faith.[12] It is summarized in the statement of Habakkuk 2:4 and repeated in the New Testament (Rom. 1:17; Gal. 3:11; Heb. 10:38): "The just shall live by faith." This is the principle by which all saints, in both Old and New Testaments, were accounted righteous in God's sight.

The principle of submissive faith is the means by which we are justified. According to Galatians 3:10,11, justification does not come from the works of law, but through a submissive faith. This is supported by the quotation of Habakkuk 2:4. Faith is the fundamental principle of justi-fication, but this faith is not one that is alone. It is a faith that submits. Its a faith that obeys. Galatians 3:26,27 states that we are accounted children of God through faith because we have put on Christ in baptism. The emphasis is on Christ, not baptism. But baptism is the means by which, or the context in which, faith embraces Christ; where faith submits to Christ.

Baptism is an act of faith through which we are united with Christ. It is not an act of merit. It earns nothing. On the contrary, it receives everything because through it we are united with Christ and his benefits. Baptism is the expression of submissive faith by which we receive God's gift of righteousness. In baptism we passively receive God's gift rather than actively earn it. In this sense, baptism is not our work, but God's work. Luther himself effectively summarized this perspective in his *Large Cat-echism*. He writes:

> Yes, it is true that our works are of no use for salvation. Baptism, however, is not our work but God's . . . God's works, however, are salutary and necessary for salvation, and they do not exclude but rather demand faith, for without faith they could not be grasped . . . it becomes beneficial to you if you accept it as God's command and ordinance, so that, baptized in the name of God, you may receive in the water the promised salvation . . .
>
> Thus you see plainly that baptism is not a work which we do but is a treasure which God gives us and faith grasps.[13]

Baptism, for Luther, was the objective mark of assurance.[14] Whenever "our sins and conscience oppress us," he writes, "we must retort, 'But I am baptized! And if I am baptized, I have the promise that I shall be saved and have eternal life, both in soul and body.' "[15] When we doubt our assurance, we can look back to the moment of our baptism and remember God's promise to us; and if we continue in the same faith that led us to obey God's word and receive the promise, then we can be assured of our present salvation because we believe the promise and the faithfulness of God to his promises.

The principle of submissive faith is also the means by which we are sanctified. The process of sanctification is rooted in faith. Our good works are works of faith; they flow from faith (1 Thess. 1:3). The best illustration of this is the "roll call" of faith in Hebrews 11. At the head of that chapter is the quotation of Habakkuk 2:4 in 10:38. It is not those who "shrink back," the Hebrew writer says, but "those who believe" that are saved (Heb. 10:39). That saving faith is then illustrated in chapter 11. It is a faith that obeys. It is a faith that submits to the commands of God. It is a faith that not only intellectually assents to God's existence ("believes that he is"), but also seeks to please him in every detail ("he rewards those who earnestly seek him," Hebrews 11:6).

Abraham, more than any other individual in this list, exhibited this submissive faith. He lived a faithful life by consistently submitting himself to the will of God. He lived the life of faith by believing on the promises of God. He trusted in God's faithfulness. Though his life was not without sin, even willful sin, he lived the life of submissive faith which was exhibited by his obedience to the will of God.

Sanctification, therefore, is rooted in the principle of submissive faith. This faith is exhibited in obedience, in good works. The works of personal righteousness to which we are called flow from this principle of faith. The works, then, are a sign of the genuineness of our faith.

The principle of submissive faith links justification and sanctification. There is a biblical text which, I think, summarizes the principle of submissive faith in the context of both justification and sanctification. Galatians 5:2-6 deals with both topics in the context of faith.

Anyone who attempts to be justified before God on the basis of obedience to law seeks a righteousness that is not by faith, but by works. They, then, have fallen from grace. Instead of seeking righteousness by means of an obedience to law through progressive sanctification, or by a righteousness which we have churned up for ourselves, we patiently wait for the righteousness that God will fully reveal. This is our hope. We hope for the full unveiling of God's gift of righteousness in the eschaton. Thus, we stand justified by faith and at the same time we patiently wait for our hope to be revealed.

The principle which underlies both our standing and our waiting, our justification and our sanctification, is stated in 5:6—"The only thing that counts is faith expressing itself through love." It is a loving, submissive faith that both justifies and sanctifies. It is a faith that works; a faith that loves; it is a faith that shows its genuineness by the way it works and the way it loves. Here, then, is the link between justification and sanctification.

Here also is the principle which yields full assurance. The original question I asked in this section was: If grace saves through faith (if I am justified by faith on the basis of a righteousness that is not my own), how progressive must my sanctification be in order to retain my standing before God? The question is actually misdirected. It is not a matter of how progressive my sanctification is or how much of the law I have kept well, but whether my attempts at sanctification are rooted in the proper principle, the principle of submissive faith. My sanctification is acceptable before God if it is rooted in a genuine and submissive disposition of faith. My righteous standing before God does not depend upon how righteous I am or how progressive my sanctification is. Rather, through a submissive faith I at one and the same time stand one hundred percent righteous before God's judgment seat on the basis of Christ's work, not mine, and my level of sanctification is acceptable to him as it flows from the principle of submissive faith. Good works and sanctification naturally flow from such a disposition of faith. They are evidence of the genuineness of my faith.

In this context I have full assurance. I do not doubt my faith though my faith is often an admixture of doubt. I know whom I have believed even though my belief is often mixed with unbelief.[16] The cry of the helpless father, "I believe, help my unbelief" (Mk. 9:24), characterizes my own faith. I know that I trust Christ as my Savior and I know that my intention is to submit to anything that he asks me to do, though I often have trouble doing what I know to do. It is my faith, with its submissive approach to God, that erases the doubts that arise in the context of my own sinfulness because I have received his gift of righteousness in Christ. My sin causes me to doubt, but my faith which seeks to love and serve God destroys the doubt as it looks to the merits of Christ rather than to my own level of sanctification. When I look within myself, there is always reason to doubt (my righteousness will never measure up). But when I look to Christ alone, I know that he is faithful to his promises, and God's gift of righteousness needs no contribution of merit from me. It is in that trust that my assurance is made full. May all the praise and glory and boasting be God's!

In conclusion, I call your attention to a significant passage that will not be formally addressed today. Yet, I think it is important to factor it into our discussion. Philippians 3 is a classic text for both justification and sanctification.[17]

The occasion for this text is Paul's response to some Judaizing teachers in Philippi. His thesis is that he will have no confidence in the flesh even though he has more reason than anyone else for such confidence. If anyone could claim the proper heritage, the proper zeal, and blameless obedience to God's law, it is Paul. However, Paul explicitly directs attention away from his own works, away from fleshly criteria. He gladly exchanges them for Christ. In verse 9 he explicitly states the nature of justification in words upon which we can hardly improve. He wishes "to be found in [Christ], not having a righteousness of my own that comes from the law, but that which is through faith in Christ—the righteousness that comes from God and is by faith." Thus, the ground of his justification is not the personal righteousness which he achieved by obedience to God's law, but rather the righteousness which he received as a gift from God through faith in Christ.

Verse 10 concerns the process of sanctification. Paul yearns to know the power of Christ's resurrection and the fellowship of Christ's suffering in his life. Through this life of power and suffering he hopes to reach the goal: glorification through the resurrection from the dead. Paul does not make sanctification a condition of his justification. He knows his sanctification is incomplete; he knows he is not perfect (v.12). He does not stand before God on the basis of how progressive his sanctification is. He struggles to "press on" so as to "take hold of that for which Christ Jesus took hold" of him. The goal is before him, and yet he knows that he falls short of it. But his confidence does not lie in his "pressing on" but in Christ Jesus who has already secured it for him. At his death, Paul will be found in Christ, and it is by that righteousness he will be saved, and not by the level of his own sanctification.

The meaning of Philippians 3 is wonderfully summarized by David Lipscomb in his Gospel Advocate commentary. He recognizes that the divine gift of righteousness is necessary if we are to have any assurance before God. He writes:

Even when a man's heart is purified by faith, and his affections all reach out towards God and seek conformity to the life of God it is imperfect. His practice of the righteousness of God falls far short of the divine standard. The flesh is weak, and the law of sin reigns in our members; so that we fall short of the perfect standard of righteousness; but if we trust God implicitly and faithfully endeavor to do his will, he knows our frame, knows our weaknesses, and as a father pities his children, so the Lord pities our infirmities and weaknesses, and imputes to us the righteousness of Christ. So Jesus stands as our justification and our righteousness, and our life is hid with Christ in God.[18]

Our standing before God is dependent upon God's gift of righteousness in Jesus Christ. We struggle for perfection, but we do not attain it. However, in Christ we stand perfect before God through faith; through a faith that is submissive and "faithfully endeavors" to do the will of God. Our confidence, then, is not in the flesh or in our works or in our blamelessness before the standard of God's righteousness. Our confidence is in Christ who is ours through submissive faith. Christ stands in our place.

Paul contrasts two approaches toward salvation in this text. The distinction between them is the distinction between the gospel and legalism. Will we boast in the flesh or in Christ? When you lay your head on your pillow at night, in what do you boast for your assurance? Are you assured because you can list the good works you performed that day, or because you are confident about the level of your sanctification, or perhaps because you have just performed an act of penitential prayer that takes care of you for the night provided you do not sin before you fall asleep? Or, are you assured because you boast only in Christ and know that your flesh is too deficient to sustain any kind of boast before God? My assurance rests in Christ and not in myself. I will boast in Christ, not in the flesh. As Paul wrote in Galatians 6:14, "May I never boast except in the cross of our Lord Jesus Christ."

Our assurance, then, is not rooted in whether we have been good enough, or whether we have reached a certain level of sanctification, or whether we have done enough. Our assurance is based on God's promise in Christ which we have received through his inspired word. God says: "If you will believe in Jesus and enter a relationship with me through baptism, then I will account you righteous. If you will submit your life to me and continue to trust in my Son throughout your life, then you can be confident of your salvation." This confidence is conveyed to us weekly when we commune with Christ in the Lord's supper where we are assured by faith that Christ is ours as surely as the bread is eaten. The cross is our boast; it alone is the ground of our salvation. Baptism and the Lord's supper are our objective means of faith.

God has given his church two objective markers of his love for us—baptism and the Lord's supper. When we approach the cross through submissive faith in the context of baptism and the Lord's supper, then we are assured of our relationship to God. We have God's promise, and God is faithful to his promises. Baptism initiates our covenantal relationship with God, and the Lord's supper is its weekly renewal. Both events point us to Christ and not ourselves as the ground of our salvation. They point us to his death and resurrection as the basis on which we are accounted righteous in God's sight. In faith, we submit to the cross of Christ and receive the promise. In the full assurance of faith, having our bodies washed and our hearts sprinkled from an evil conscience, we draw near to God.

We are not pilgrims uncertain of our prospects. Our assurance does not rest upon the conjectures of the medieval pilgrim. Our assurance rests in the promise of God who accounts us righteous in Christ Jesus through submissive faith. We are pilgrims, but pilgrims certain of our home; certain that "when the roll is called up yonder," we'll be there.

Endnotes

1. *The Trial of Jeanne d'Arc*, trans. W. P. Barrett (New York, 1932), pp.320-321 as quoted by Steven Ozment, *The Age of Reform, 1250-1550 An Intellectual and Religious History of Late Medieval and Reformation Europe* (New Haven: Yale University Press, 1980), pp.30-31.

2. Ozment, p.31.

3. "The *viator* [pilgrim] cannot have a subjective certitude of salvation," Heiko A. Oberman, *The Harvest of Medieval Theology: Gabriel Briel and Late Hedieval Nominalism* (Cambridge, MA: Harvard University Press, 1963), p. 227.

4. This is a theme articulated by Oberman and Ozment to whom I am indebted. See particularly Ozment, *The Age of Reform*, pp.204-222 and *The Reformation in the Cities* (New Haven: Yale University Press, 1975), pp.15-46; Bernd Moeller, "Piety in Germany Around 1500," in *The Reformation in Medieval Perspective*, ed. Steven Ozment (Chicago: University of Chicago Press, 1971), pp.50-75; and Thomas N. Tentler, *Sin and Confession on the Eve of the Reformation* (Princeton: Princeton University Press, 1977) with Ozment's review in *The Journal of Religion* 58 (1978), pp.205-206.

5. This section was my summary of the theology that is outlined in Oberman's classic book *Harvest*. The reader who is interested might note in particular pages 175-178 for a summary of the nominalist doctrine of justification.

6. As quoted by James M. Kittleson, *Luther the Reformer: The Story of the Man and His Career* (Minneapolis: Augsburg, 1985), p.56.

7. He wrote: "I was indeed a pious monk and kept the rules of my order so strictly that I can say: if ever a monk gained heaven through monkery, it should have been I. All my monastic brethren who knew me will testify to this. I would have martyred myself to death with fasting, praying, reading, and other good works had I remained a monk much longer" (as quoted by Hans J. Hillerbrand, *The Reformation* [Grand Rapids; Baker, 1978], p.24).

8. Luther, "On Two Kinds of Righteousness," in *Martin Luther: Selections from his Writings*, ed. John Dillenberger (Garden City: Doubleday, 1961), pp.86-96.

9. I recognize that sometimes "sanctify" is used in a definitive sense that overlaps or is virtually synonymous with justification. However, here I am referring to the progressive sense of sanctification which refers to our life of faith in Christ where we seek to be more and more conformed to his image. For the distinction, see John Murray, *Collected Writings of John Murray* (Edinburgh: The Banner of Truth Trust, 1977), 2:277-319.

10. Hendrikus Berkhof, *Christian Faith: An Introduction to the Study of the Faith*, trans. by Sierd Woudstra (Grand Rapids: Eerdmans, 1979), pp.453-454. See also the balanced and historically conscious discussion of Otto Weber, *Foundation of Dogmatics*, trans. and annotated by Darrell L. Guder (Grand Rapids: Eerdmans, 1983), 2:315-329.

11. In *Luther's Works*, v.47 (Saint Louis: Concordia Publishing House, 1959).

12. Perhaps this could be called "obedient faith" (Rom. 1:5; 16:26), but I hesitate to use this biblical phrase because of the way in which it might be understood. If I understand "obedient faith" as my obligation to obey a certain percentage of the law in my sanctification in order to be saved, then this would return to a legalistic concept of faith. However, "obedient faith" can be thought of as a synonym for my expression if it is given the definition that I will shortly attach to it.

13. Luther, "Large Catechism," in *The Book of Concord: The Confessions of the Evangelical Lutheran Church*, trans. and ed. by Theodore G. Tappert (Philadelphia: Fortress Press, 1959), p.441. Alexander Campbell also expresses a similar sentiment (*Millennial Harbinger* 6 [1835], pp.83-84): "Others think that when they have been immersed they have *done* something worthy of praise. He that is immersed does nothing any more than he who is buried. In immersion, as in being born, and in being buried, the subject is always passive."

14. This is exactly Campbell's point. Baptism is an objective seal of God's promise to forgive us. Assurance, then, does not simply depend upon a movement of one's feelings, but rests in a "sensible" event—we know when we were saved. Cf. *Christian Baptist* 5 (1828), pp.254-255.

15. Luther, "Large Catechism," p.442.

16.   John Calvin, *Institutes of the Christian Religion,* Vol.20, *LCC,* trans. by Ford Lewis Battles and edited by J. T. McNeill (Philadelphia: Westminster Press, 1960), 3.2.17/562: "Surely, while we teach that faith ought to be certain and assured, we cannot imagine any certainty that is not tinged with doubt, or any assurance that is not assailed by some anxiety . . . we say that believers are in a perpetual conflict with their own unbelief. Far, indeed, are we from putting their consciences in any peaceful repose, undisturbed by any tumult at all."

17.   An excellent and recent commentary on this text which coincides with my perspective is Moisés Silva, *Philippians, WEC* (Chicago: Moody Press, 1988), pp.177-195.

18.   David Lipscomb, *Ephesians, Philippians, and Colossians,* Vol. 4 *A Commentary on the New Testament Epistles,* edited, with additional notes by J. W. Shepherd (Nashville: Gospel Advocate, 1957), pp.205-206.

Richard Earl Oster, Jr.

Richard Oster has served as Professor of New Testament at Harding University Graduate School of Religion since 1978. During that time he has also served as Adjunct Faculty at Rhodes College in Memphis. From 1977 to 1978, he served as Adjunct Faculty at the University of Houston. Prior to that he was a Teaching Fellow at Princeton Theological Seminary (1971-1974).

He received the B.A. from Texas Tech University (1969), the M.A. from Rice University (1971), and the Ph.D. (magna cum laude) from Princeton Theological Seminary (1974). He has since engaged in independent research at Franz J. Dölger-Institut an der Universität Bonn and independent study at the Österreichisches Archäologisches Institut in Vienna, Austria.

Writings include two books: *A Bibliography on Ancient Ephesus; With Introduction and Index* and *The Acts of the Apostles*. Articles have appeared in *Restoration Quarterly, Harvard Theological Review, Journal of Biblical Literature, Encyclopedia of Early Christianity* and many others. Published reviews include J. Christiaan Beker's *Paul the Apostle: The triumph of God in Life and Thought,* Jack Finegan's *Archaeological History of the Ancient Middle East,* and Edwin Yamauchi's *The Archaeology of New Testament Cities in Western Asia Minor.*

Richard is a member of many professional societies. Among them are Studiorum Novi Testamenti Societas, Society of Biblical Literature, and Society for Ancient Numismatics.

Grace and Works in Ephesians 2:1-10 and Titus 2:11-14

Richard Oster

Since we are living in the midst of an acknowledged disintegration of the doctrinal consensus of the churches of Christ, it behooves me to say a few words about my exegetical assumptions for interpreting the text of Scripture assigned to me for today.

Scripture texts are best understood when they are read in the contexts of the occasions to which they were addressed. Words and phrases often have many potential meanings and one's hope of arriving at the most correct interpretation is greatly enhanced when the words and phrases of Scripture are viewed in both the grammatical context of the sentence in which they occur as well as in the broader occasional context of the epistle. For example: I cannot know if Mr. Smith is lenient or strict if I only overhear Mr. Smith say to his son, "I'll ground you for an entire month if I ever catch you doing that again," unless I know what the son has done. I cannot know if Mr. Smith is harsh or compassionate if I only overhear Mr. Smith say to his wife, "What you have done has broken my heart, but I forgive you," unless I know what Mrs. Smith has done.

So it is with the acts and statements of God in these Scriptures. We must be aware of the context to which God's statements are injected. We must carefully analyze biblical statements about grace, works, and faith and their relationship in the specific context in which they were addressed. For example, you cannot always assume that the treatment of this in Romans was addressed to the same context as the treatment in the book of Hebrews or the epistle to the Galatians. Even a cursory look at a concordance or a Greek language lexicon shows that the meanings of Greek words vary, not only from author to author, but also from epistle to epistle, and even from section to section within an epistle. We should always ask the question: "What was the issue to which these words of God we spoken?" Truth, it seems to me, is never served by merely gathering word occurrences from a concordance without giving adequate attention to what particular doctrinal aberration is being addressed by the authors of Scripture.

A clear example of the need to interpret verses in their larger context is seen in the fact that Paul is comfortable with believers keeping "religious days" in Romans 14:5-8 while he pronounces a condemnation on believers who keep "religious days" in Galatians 4:10,11. How should one interpret this diversity within Pauline teaching? Some are apparently ignorant of the diversity within Paul on this point. Others simply pick the verses which best suit their own doctrinal outlook and dismiss the other verses. My own advice is that rather than getting involved in special pleading to neutralize particular verses you are uncomfortable with, the student of the Scriptures should first investigate all of the relevant verses, each in its own distinct context, and then begin to discover the reasons for the diversities seen in them. Beneath the diversity of special occasions and contingent situations in Paul, one will discover, I believe, a coherent and consistent doctrinal and spiritual outlook within Paul.

Now we turn to Ephesians 2. The occasion for Paul's letter to the Ephesians is a situation in which believers, primarily Gentile ones (2:11 and 3:1), needed to be urged to bring their ethical behavior into line with their spiritual condition and commitments. They needed to become what they were. In Paul's words in 4:1, they needed to live a life worthy of the calling to which they had been called (4:1). The term Paul uses in 4:1 that is translated variously—"I beg you," "I beseech you," "I urge you"—is *parakalo*, a Greek term often used to underscore the main theme or the main point of a Greek epistle or petition. In light of this, the epistle to the Ephesians should be divided into two parts with 4:1 serving as the hinge verse. The first part of the letter (chapters 1-3) establishes the nature and the characteristics of the calling which comes from God, while the second part (chapters 4-6) spells out in the context of the Ephesian setting what a life and walk carried on worthily before God should look like. So the point is, there are two halves to the letter. The summary is in 4:1, "lead a life worthy of the calling." Chapters 1-3 spell out what the calling is, and chapters 4-6 spell out what the worthy walk looks like, and 4:1 is the hinge verse.

What we are about to see in Ephesians is Paul's strategy for moving this community of faith into a more responsible manner of living a godly life. The basic structure and outline of the epistle is used to accomplish this goal by following the frequent scriptural paradigm of presenting to the hearer first what God has done in his prevenient and lavish grace and then telling the hearer what God expects, indeed demands, as a response. This is a very frequent pattern in Scripture and it is obviously there in the book of Acts. This two-prong strategy of beginning with a statement about the gracious acts of God followed up by the lifestyle that God expects in return can even be shown in the epistle to the Ephesians through some of the grammatical characteristics of the epistle. In chapter 1-3, one encounters an emphasis upon indicative verbs, that is, statements about what God has done and continues to do in the lives of the saints, with only one occurrence of an imperative verb (2:11). Paul is not in a hurry to get to the requirements that God places upon us until he first emphasizes what God has already done on our behalf.

Now in contrast to that, the second half of the epistle contains approximately forty occurrences of imperative verbs, statements about what God demands from us in response to his saving grace. The fact that the predominant emphasis in the first half of the epistle is upon what God has already done prior to and apart from our own works is reflected in the statements of some of the major sub-sections such as the blessing section of 1:3-14 and the prayer sections in 1:15-22 and 3:14-21. And all I'm trying to emphasize here is that if you look at some of the major units of thought in this first half of the epistle, you will see again and again the emphasis that Paul is trying to give in this section is to stress what God has done for us without yet laying any responsibilities upon the readership. So, for example 1:3-14, you basically find statements where God is the subject of the verb or the participle and it narrates what he has done for us, how he has forgiven us, how he has predestined us and how he has revealed himself to us.

In the prayer sections, you have two of these in the first three chapters—the first one is 1:15-22. You notice there he prays that God will give them greater spiritual insight, that is verse 17, and the content of the spiritual insight is so that they will better understand what God has done for them. So, here again you see in the prayer section this emphasis on what Paul wants really to nail down is their increased appreciation for what God has done and not so much yet on what they are to do in response.

And then finally in 3:14ff, the petition—or the prayer—focuses on the things that God is doing and Paul hopes that God will do in the life of the believer: Be strengthened with might through his spirit in the inner man, Christ dwell in your hearts through faith, rooted and grounded in love, have power to understand what God has done for you in his love. So even the major subsections of these first three chapters again drive home the point that the emphasis is on the indicative, statements about what God has done for the people.

It is quite instructive to us and extremely revealing of Paul's strategy that even though the church at Ephesus contains liars, fornicators, thieves, etcetera, his prayer is not that this sinful behavior stop. Now if you want to get a profile of the Ephesian church, you get that from reading the last three chapters where Paul says through many imperatives that they need to quit doing certain kinds of behavior. For example, those who are in the church that steal, should steal no more. I'm assuming all of that is said because, in fact, some of them are doing it. And so you get a picture here of a church that can compete with Corinth in terms of a moral profile.

But what is so significant is that, in light of Paul's knowledge already in the prayer in chapters 1 and 3 of this condition, his prayer is not something like: "God, please stop all this fornication" or "punish the liars" or something like that. His prayer is not a direct attack upon the symptomatic problem of sinful living. Paul's intercessory petition for the Ephesians—these would be the intercessory prayers in 1:15ff and 3:14ff—is that they better understand, that the Ephesians better understand, both what God has done for them and how great is the divine power which is available through the indwelling of the Spirit of God. Paul believed, at least in the setting of the Ephesian church, that better behavior among the saints would eventuate when believers better understood what God had done for them. Needless to say, this scriptural strategy has not always been followed in the life of the church. When you see a church that has the problems depicted in the last three chapters, throughout church history people have often taken other routes to try to correct those problems.

I must point out that the order of first giving the indicative statements and then presenting the covenant imperatives is no accident. John says this most clearly in the simple statement that we love because—that is, connecting the two—we love *because* he *first* loved us. To tamper with the sequence of this order, in my opinion, is to tamper with the very heart and nature of scriptural faith and the truth of the gospel. To put the imperatives first as though they both preceded and established the conditions of God's gracious acts is the most diabolical kind of works-righteousness. For Paul, the only acceptable righteousness is one that comes from God and is appropriated by faith. God's love for the sinful world was not in response to anything, imperatives or otherwise, which I or anyone else did to catch God's attention or to win his love.

On the other hand, merely to proclaim the indicative statements of God's sovereign acts of grace in Christ with no reference to the responsibility and the accountability which comes with the embracing of grace and its blessing is a betrayal of the entire pattern of Scripture. The parable of the unmerciful servant (Matt. 18:21ff) should have established once for all the fact that gracious treatment from God demands gracious behavior from the recipients. My point is, while it is erroneous to leave the impression that the way you get the grace of God is by first obeying a bunch of imperatives and somehow earn it, it is equally irresponsible to say, "Well, God has done these things for us and now we can just do what we wish." Both of those are options people have taken in the history of Christianity, and it seems as though Matthew 18:21, in the parable of the unmerciful servant, indicates that here is a person who has received grace from the king and parabolically is saved but does not know how to transmit that and incorporate that in his own life and so he beats up his fellow servant. You know how the story ends. He is put in jail forever.

This is, of course, the very import of Ephesians 4:31-5:1 where Paul writes:

> Let all bitterness and wrath and anger and clamor and slander be put away from you, with all malice, and be kind to one another, tenderhearted, forgiving one another, as God in Christ forgave you. Therefore be imitators of God as beloved children.

So three imperatives are found in this section, 4:31-5:1. The imperative of "let all these bad behaviors be put away," is one of the imperatives. And then the imperative to be kind and the imperative to be imitators. You have three examples in 4:31-5:1 where the foundation of the imperatives come from. This is the way God has treated you; therefore, you are commanded to live this way. And, of course, that is logically impossible if you do not know how God has treated you. You cannot pass on what you have not received.

Turning now to Ephesians 2, I intend to focus my thoughts primarily on verses 8-10, since I believe that these verses can serve as a summary statement of Paul's entire strategy reflected in the epistle as a whole. I am not saying that these are Paul's summary statements, but I think those verses serve as a summary statement. The Greek word *charis* translated *grace* in Ephesians 2:8 is a term with many nuances in the epistle to the Ephesians. It is not only the good favor of God through which a condition of salvation is established, according to Ephesians 2:8, but it is also the ongoing divine favor which maintains our relationship to God. It is not enough for Paul just to tell people they received grace once, but it is part of the ongoing Christian life. For example, the epistle itself opens with the statement "grace to you and peace from God our Father and the Lord Jesus Christ." The letter ends in 6:24 with the statement "grace be with all those that love the Lord." So grace is not just something that happened once, but it really is part of the ongoing atmosphere, the spiritual atmosphere, in which the Christian walks. Paul here, in an intercessory way, is praying that this grace will be upon the Ephesians.

The grace of God is the foundation and reason for our worship and praise (1:6): "To the praise of his glorious grace which he freely bestowed on us in the beloved" as well as our treatment of fellow believers (4:32), which we looked at just a moment ago. Twice Paul mentions the wealth and riches of God's grace (1:7): "In him we have redemption through his blood, the forgiveness of our trespasses according to the riches of his grace." And then in 2:7: "That in the coming ages he might show the immeasurable riches of his grace in kindness toward us in Christ Jesus." And once Paul mentions that *charis* 'grace' can be communicated to other believers through godly speech (4:29): "Let no evil talk come out of your mouths, but only such as is good for edification as it befits the occasion that it may impart grace to those who hear it."

A final and significant dimension of *charis* or grace in Ephesians is its use to explain the power and favor of God which equips and guides both Paul's own gifts from God for his apostolic ministry and those many other gifts given by God to the church at large. When you look in 3:1-13, you will notice several times Paul's saying that it is according to the grace of God that he was given this office of apostle. And 4:7, dealing with a larger group of Christians: "But grace was given to each of us according to the measure of Christ's gift."

To those who have ears to hear, Paul makes it as clear as possible that the salvation based on grace cannot be correctly explained or understood in terms of human achievement or meritorious activity. Salvation is the gift, and as a gift, is not a loan. It is not an installment purchase to be paid back incrementally. Moreover, not only is this salvation the gift of Ephesians 2:8, it is a gift *from God*. It is neither a gift from a brotherhood nor from a church; it is a gift of God. Since this salvation is by grace, it is false to teach or think that it arises from or consists of human works and human behavior. It seems to me that Paul is trying to make an emphatic point when he states that this salvation is not of ourselves, nor is it of works since God is not the kind of God who gave gifts based upon objective human merit, then he can make us alive together with Christ when we were dead spiritually (2:6,7), and can hardly bestow forgiveness upon us while we were in our sins and trespasses (1:7,8). The good news of the gospel as I understand it is *not* that God decided to overlook a few defects in us, but rather that he forgave our defection from him. Advocates of moralistic works-righteousness will always find a way to squirm around and justify themselves by acknowledging an occasional defect. A regenerate sinner will always acknowledge his own past defections and former loyalty to the flesh.

It is with the prepositional phrase "through faith" in Ephesians 2:8, that Paul highlights what we would call the human component, or the human part in the process of salvation. This is a clear reference to the necessary, *but never meritorious*, place of a person's trust in God, a trust which appropriates salvation in Christ. Other Ephesian texts which point to the importance of a personal trust for the life of the child of God include 3:11,12 which reads: "This was according to the eternal purpose which he realized in Christ Jesus our Lord in whom we have boldness and confidence of access through our faith in him," and 3:17 which states "that Christ may dwell in your hearts through faith."

While the Calvinistic position of "the gift of faith" to the elect flies in the face of the evidence of the conversion stories of Acts and Paul's own writings, one should be careful not to throw out the proverbial baby with the bath water. Paul indeed does know of the gift of faith given to *believers.* Once one receives the personal indwelling of God's Spirit in obedience to the gospel, then the same Holy Spirit ministers to believers, assists them in sanctification, administers gifts, and bears its own fruit in the believer's life with God. One of the manifestations of this is the giving of *pistis*—and that can be translated *faith, faithfulness*—to the believer. The idea of *pistis* being given by God to believers is seen in differing contexts and texts such as Romans 12:3, Galatians 5:22, and Ephesians 6:23. The Ephesian text reads: "Love with faith from God our Father and the Lord Jesus Christ." This "givenness" of *pistis* should come as no surprise to students of Paul, since Paul also taught the givenness of *agape* to God's children through the ministry of the Holy Spirit of God. Not only is this one of the fruits of the Spirit as you know from Galatians 5:22; but also in Romans 5:5 Paul writes: "Hope does not disappoint us because God's love [that is, *agape*] has been poured into our hearts through the Holy Spirit which has been given to us."

Moving on in the Ephesian text, the reason that God will not tolerate religious attitudes of self-sufficiency in works-righteousness is because they inevitably lead to boasting. This is the reason God set it up this way, that it is based on grace and it is not of ourselves, because he does not want to put up with a bunch of boasting, arrogant, self-righteous people. He has enough problems. A boasting heart is a guaranteed way to undermine a proper relationship with God. God hates pride and quite clearly fights against his own people when their hearts and activities demonstrate a holier-than-thou spirituality and self-assured works-righteousness. If you think not, just reread the parable about two people who prayed at the Temple (Luke 18:9-14).

In Ephesians 2:10, we finally encounter the phrase "for good works" and see very clearly the place and function of these in God's scheme of redemption. It seems to me that one should identify the specific content of these good works by looking within the epistle of the Ephesians itself. While the term "good works" in and of itself can refer to many ideas in the Bible, the "good works" of Ephesians 2:8-10 which Paul wants the saints to walk in are those, I believe, mentioned in Ephesians 4, 5, and 6. With the reference to "good works" in 2:10, it is now possible to explore the place of works in the life of the believer. The conceptual and doctrinal background to Ephesians 2:10 in this regard is the wide spread biblical notion of predestination and election. Paul had earlier mentioned in Ephesians the doctrinal precepts of predestination and election in 1:4-6. A central component of Paul's doctrine of predestination and election which he takes from the Old Testament, the call of Abraham, Genesis 12, is that God's predestination and election of people are always based upon grace and that they are accomplished for a greater goal. Thus, when God chose Abraham, it was not with the idea in mind of blessing Abraham just for the sake of blessing Abraham. Abraham was chosen and blessed by God so that he could become a channel of God's blessings to other families and nations of the earth.

Since God's choice of Abraham was not based upon Abraham's prior merit or righteousness, one must conclude that God chose Abraham because God wanted to choose Abraham. Stated in its simplest terms, part of the job description of being God is you get to do what you please. Psalm 115:3 and Psalm 135:5,6 say that. In a similar way, Paul affirms in Ephesians 1:5,9 that God's election of those in Christ is based upon God's will and God's good pleasure.

One of the occupational hazards of being the elect both in Judaism and Christianity is you think you were elected because you are so good and worthwhile. In reality, the reason God chose a people was for a greater goal or purpose, and this point is quite clear in Ephesians 1:4. For example, Paul says that we were chosen, we were elected, before the foundation of the earth *in order to be* holy and blameless before him.

The phrase in Ephesians 1:6,12 that "we are to live for the praise of his glory" is again showing there is a greater purpose behind all of this. So my point is, that as we talk about good works, we need to see this in the theological scheme of both the Old and New Testament. God created our election and predestination so that we could perform good works in his kingdom.

Now the phrase in Ephesians 2:10, "by walking in these good works," clearly shows that Paul does not mean here just an occasional stroll. The verb *peripato*, (walk) is throughout Ephesians used to describe lifestyle. And so Paul is saying this is a lifestyle that will characterize those who are a part of God's people. Even though it is rather clear in the Scriptures that election takes place for the purpose of serving God's business in the world rather than self achievement and self aggrandizement, this is not a popular gospel today. In our own culture which is so permeated by self-serving lifestyles, by secular narcissism, by the health-and-wealth gospel, and by the what's-in-it-for-me religion, the idea of election to servanthood will not find a large audience. While baby boomers may be interested in church and religion, it is still not clear whether man will serve God for naught.

In concluding this sketch of Ephesians, we see that the purpose for which God created us in Christ Jesus was not to give God a way to acknowledge publicly the church's own moral worthiness nor was it to establish a holy huddle. The reason for which God saved and sanctified sinners was so that he could possess and guide a group of individuals made contrite by their acknowledged need for constant grace, and who would, in faith, carry out God's own agenda, in God's own way, on God's own earth. Believers were redeemed by grace according to Paul, and Paul sees "good works" as the fruit *but not the root* of one's salvation.

Finally, I want to make just one comment on some material in the later part of Ephesians. I want to say something about what Paul says about those who do not respond to his admonitions in 4:1, to live a life worthy of the calling. For those believers who would not strive in faith to live according to the holy and blameless life to which the gospel called them, Paul wrote that they faced the coming wrath of God (5:6). Since God is not mocked, they could count on the fact that if any of them continued in their pagan lifestyles, they would be treated as pagans by God for, after all, "no fornicator or impure man or one who is covetous, that is, an idolater, has any inheritance in the kingdom of Christ and of God" (Eph. 5:5). The typical Gentile convert in Roman Ephesus was probably not that much different from the typical American. Telling Americans about the demands and responsibility of grace is not any easier now than it was for Paul. We hear much more about rights than we do about responsibility in our culture. While the popular culture of the 1960s and '70s proclaimed "love means never having to say you are sorry," God said "repent or perish." While some forms of popular Christianity proclaim that love does not require anything in return, Paul's own strategy in Ephesians affirms that God's grace makes demands and places profound responsibilities upon his covenant people. That this call to good works would be set before the church makes complete sense in light of the fact that it can only be said of believers that they are "built into a temple for a dwelling place of God in the Spirit" (Eph. 2:21,22).

William Woodson

William Woodson is a professor of Bible at David Lipscomb University. From 1982 to 1990, he served as director of the graduate program in Bible at Lipscomb. Previously he served as chairman of the Bible Department at Freed-Hardeman University where he began teaching in 1959. He also served as Freed-Hardeman's lectureship director and editor of the lectureship book from 1974 to 1981.

He received the A.A. degree from Freed-Hardeman University, the B.A. from Union University, and the M.A. from Harding Graduate School of Religion. In 1968, the M.Th. was conferred upon him by New Orleans Baptist Theological Seminary. In 1973, he received the Th.D. from that institution.

William and Jeanne Creasy Woodson have three children: Melissa Ruth, Bill, and Allison. They also have five grandchildren.

Writings include *Standing for Their Faith* (1979) and *Perfecting Faith* (1982). He is co-author of *Sounding Brass and Clanging Symbols* (1991).

Grace and Works in Ephesians 2:1-10 and Titus 2:11-14

William Woodson

We shall see whether I am delighted to be here or not. At this point, I am glad to see you. I hope that this is a good day for all of us. My participation in this forum is not because I am mad at anybody. I am not here on any kind of personal vendetta. I am not here to declare anybody a heretic. I am not here to burn anybody at the stake. I am here in an investigation of truth and because I love truth and because I love people and because I love the Lord and Scripture. I am willing to be here and hope that it will be helpful to you.

By way of brief introduction: Richard, I do not know where you are, but you saved me a world of time, and I appreciate it. All right, enough of the fun; now to work. Our son Bill is here with me and I appreciate his being here and he is here to do three things: one, to flip the slides; two, to help me drive back home; and three, to patch up the wounds if any are laid upon later in the day.

All right, let us begin with the overhead. Chart number one: "Where I stand." I stand with what I was taught that

lead me to leave the Baptist faith in 1950. Until that time
I had lived and worked among the people of the Baptist
group. I spent many pleasant hours among the Baptists. I
have studied in their undergraduate and graduate schools,
read many of their books, know many of their leaders
today, and have read from several of them. And yet what I
came to believe in 1950 is absolutely what I believe today. I
have not moved from that.

Secondly, I stand with representative men among the
churches of Christ. The roll call could be extended. I
would include such men as Gus Nichols, B. C. Goodpasture,
H. A. Dixon, Franklin Camp, Frank Van Dyke, N. B.
Hardeman, Guy N. Woods, and many, many others. They
have taught and upheld these same principles for generations. These same principles are upheld by many faithful

---

Chart #1

PERSONAL COMMENTS

My participation is not a personal attack on anyone.

WHERE I STAND

1. With what I was taught which led me from the
Baptist faith in 1950.

2. With what representative men among churches
of Christ [Such as: Gus Nichols, B. C. Goodpasture,
H. A. Dixon, Franklin Camp, Frank Van Dyke, N. B.
Hardeman, Guy N. Woods, and many others] have taught
and upheld for generations; and which many faithful men
and women still teach and uphold.

3. Those who are now teaching salvation by grace
alone through faith alone have moved away from the
faith and practice of churches of Christ. It is they, and not
I, who are obliged to show why they have left the positions our brethren have maintained.

men and women today. Those who are now teaching salvation by grace alone, through faith alone, among us have moved away from the faith and practice of churches of Christ. It is they, and not I, who are obliged to show why they have left the positions our brethren have maintained.

Chart #2

What I DO NOT BELIEVE:

(1) I DO NOT BELIEVE: men are saved by the law of Moses, but by the gospel of Christ.

(2) I DO NOT BELIEVE: men are saved by their own righteousness.

(3) I DO NOT BELIEVE: men are able to earn salvation, merit salvation, or purchase salvation by any action or effort on their part.

(4) I DO NOT BELIEVE: men are obliged to "do enough" to earn or merit salvation.

Chart number two: "What I do not believe." I do not believe that we are saved by the law of Moses, that we are saved by the works of Roman Catholicism, by the works of medieval theology. These are false religions. I do not believe in works of supererogation. I do not believe that men are saved by their own righteousness. I do not believe that men are able to earn salvation, to merit salvation, to purchase salvation by any action or any effort on their part.

I do not believe that men are obliged to "do enough" to earn or merit salvation.

[Chart #3.] Third: "What I do believe." I do believe that the gospel of Christ is the means and the only means whereby we can learn what to do to be saved from sin. I am not here to defend Roman Catholicism, Protestant theology, Calvinism of the hyper-nature or the modified nature, either the five-step, four-step, or three-step, to use the terms in Lordship salvation discussion. I am not here to defend Lutheranism or reformed theology.

I do believe there are two kinds of works mentioned in the New Testament. There are works which are excluded from the means of our salvation. They are works of human invention, human merit, works that enable boasting, and the works of the law of Moses.

There are works, in the second place, of obedience to God as guided by the gospel so the sinner can become a child of God by God's grace.

There are also works which the child of God is to do to remain saved, and to remain saved also by the grace of God. I believe the salvation of the sinner is by the grace of

---

Chart #3

WHAT I DO BELIEVE

(1) I DO BELIEVE: The gospel of Christ is the means and the only means whereby we can can learn what to do to be saved from sin.

(2) I DO BELIEVE: There are two kinds of "WORKS" mentioned in the New Testament:

(a) There are works which are excluded from the means of our salvation. They are works of human invention, merit, works which enable boasting, and works of the law of Moses.

(b) There are works of obedience to God as guided by the gospel so the sinner can become a child of God by God's grace. There are also works which the child of God is to do to remain saved, also by the grace of God.

(3) I DO BELIEVE: The salvation of the sinner is by the grace of God; the salvation of the faithful Christian is by the grace of God.

God and the salvation of the faithful Christian is by the grace of God.

Now the text with which we are concerned. [Chart #4.] Notice the English translation for those who are unable to study the Greek; but the two are the same. The King James: "For by grace are ye saved through faith." ASV: "For by grace have ye been saved . . . ," and so on. I call attention to the underlining of *chariti este sesosmenoi* which will have a significant part in this discussion. It is underlined, I believe, here. And in the next place, in verse 8, *te gar chariti este sesosmenoi dia pisteos.* This will be

---

Chart #4

EPHESIANS 2:8-10

"For by grace are ye saved through faith" (KJV)
"For by grace have ye been saved through faith" (ASV)
"For by grace you have been saved through faith" (RSV)
"For it is by grace that you have been saved, through faith" (NIV)

"Yes, it is by His grace that you have been saved, by the exercise of faith" (F. F. Bruce)

Nestle, <u>Novum</u> <u>Testamentum</u>
Ephesians 2:6-10
Προς Εφεσιους

Χριστῷ, — χάριτί ἐστε σεσωσμένοι, — καὶ συνήγειρεν καὶ συνεκάθισεν ἐν τοῖς ἐπουρανίοις ἐν Χριστῷ Ἰησοῦ, ἵνα ἐνδείξηται ἐν τοῖς αἰῶσιν τοῖς ἐπερχομένοις τὸ ὑπερβάλλον πλοῦτος τῆς χάριτος αὐτοῦ ἐν χρηστότητι ἐφ' ἡμᾶς ἐν Χριστῷ Ἰησοῦ. τῇ γὰρ χάριτί ἐστε σεσωσμένοι διὰ πίστεως· καὶ τοῦτο οὐκ ἐξ ὑμῶν, θεοῦ τὸ δῶρον· οὐκ ἐξ ἔργων, ἵνα μή τις καυχήσηται. αὐτοῦ γάρ ἐσμεν ποίημα, κτισθέντες ἐν Χριστῷ Ἰησοῦ ἐπὶ ἔργοις ἀγαθοῖς, οἷς προητοίμασεν ὁ θεὸς ἵνα ἐν αὐτοῖς περιπατήσωμεν.

crucial. Notice particularly *este sesosmenoi*.

In the next place I want to call attention to the word *dia*. *Dia* is the word that is translated 'through'. [Chart #5.] Notice A. T. Robertson's statement here. (*Dia* is the agent.) "The agent is conceived as coming between the non-attainment and the attainment of the object in view." Notice that point: non-attainment, attainment. Between the two is *dia*. "Abstract ideas are frequently so expressed" . . . as the passage we are looking at.

Chart #5

Concerning δια with the genitive

<u>A. T. Robertson</u>

". . . the agent is conceived as coming between the non-attainment and the attainment of the object in view. . . . Abstract ides are frequently so expressed as σεσωσμενοι δια πιστεως" (Eph. 2:8).

A. T. Robertson, <u>Grammar of the Greek NT in the Light of Historical Research</u> (1934), p.582.

[Chart #6.] George Benedict Winer: "In Ephesians 2:8, *dia pisteos* [expresses] the subjective means."

[Chart #7.] Now notice: Occasions of *dia*. I call attention on the left hand to the verse, in the middle, the expression with *dia*, and on the right hand, the agent or means. Ephesians 2:8, "saved" *dia pisteos* 'through faith.' Romans 6, "buried with him through baptism." In Galatians 3:26, "children of God through faith, for you were baptized into Christ." Titus 3:5, "You were saved by (through) the washing of regeneration." First Peter 3:21, "souls were saved through water." Attention is called to the fact that *dia* in 2:8 is the same word that is used in these others. Question: If you cannot eliminate *dia pisteos* 'though faith', how can you eliminate *dia baptismos*

Chart #6

<u>G. B. Winer</u>

"But in E. 2.8 . . . δια πιστεως [expresses] the subjective means."

G. B. Winer, <u>A</u> <u>Treatise</u> <u>on</u> <u>the</u> <u>NT</u> <u>Greek</u>, Translator W. F. Moulton (1882), page 272.

'through baptism'? How can you eliminate the washing of regeneration?

In the next place, I call attention to Mark 16:16. We may get into it later. I want to notice the aorist participle. That may come up for further discussion. Notice: "He that believeth and is baptized shall be saved."

Notice in the next place, "only,"—and this will come up—carefully. [Chart #8.] I call attention to the word *only*, the Greek word *monos*, or in the neuter, *monon*. The word in the neuter means "alone," "only," "merely." It is, I think, quite significant to notice the Septuagint in Genesis 2:18: "God said, It is not good for the man to be *monon*, 'only, alone.' Question: Was there anybody else on earth besides Adam? Who was it? Now, *monon* is exactly what Adam was when God said that word. Notice in James 2:24: "Not by faith *monon*." We will discuss that perhaps in some detail.

Now, I call attention to some matters concerning this business of salvation by faith.

First, outside our own brotherhood. I refer particularly to a man by the name of Livingston Blauvelt. [Chart #9.] You have the references here. It has to do with what is called "Lordship salvation." Lordship salvation entails the idea that "one must trust Jesus Christ as his Savior from sin and must also commit himself to Christ as Lord of his life." Blauvelt says that is wrong. Why? He says this

Chart #7
Occurrences of dia

Verse	Expression with δια	Agent, Means
Eph. 2:8	εστε σεσωσμενοι [are ye saved]	δια πιστεως [through faith]
Rom. 6:4	συνεταφημεν αυτω [we are buried with him]	δια της βαπτισματος [through baptism] [into death]
Gal. 3:26 27	υιοι του θεου εστε [ye are children of God]	δια πιστεως γαρ εις Χριστον εβαπτισθετε [by faith] [for into Christ ye were baptized]
Titus 3:5	εσωσεν ημεις [he saved us]	δια λουτρου παλιγγενεσιας [by the washing of regeneration]
1 Pet. 3:20	ψυχαι διεσωθησαν [souls were saved]	δια υδατος [by water]
Mark 16:16	ο πιστευσαντες και βαπτισθεις He that believeth and is baptized]	σωθησεται [shall be saved]

teaching "is false because it subtly adds works to the clear and simple condition for salvation." "An unbeliever . . . must only accept him as his own personal Savior." "Salvation is always by faith alone. People can do nothing to

---

Chart #8

Concerning "only" μονος

"1. an adjective, alone (without a companion) . . . "

"2. Neut. μονον as adv., alone, only, merely"
Thayer, Lexicon, p.418.

Gen. 2:18 "ου καλον ειναι τον ανθροπον μονον", LXX

"It is not good that the man should be alone: [ASV]

James 2:24 "ουκ εκ πιστεως μονον"
[not by faith only]

---

merit God's gift of salvation, including making Jesus Christ
Lord of their lives." He is understanding faith only to
exclude "Jesus is Lord."

Further, "justification is God's act of declaring a believer righteous at the moment he believes in Christ"—"*at
the moment*"! Notice in the next place. "The question:
Must one knowledgeably accept by faith Jesus as Lord in
order to be saved, has already been answered in the negative." My point: Does faith only exclude the necessity of
believing Jesus is Lord? Outside of our brotherhood, it is
so affirmed.

Notice the statement from Ryrie. This may come up
later. "The message of faith only and the message of faith
plus commitment cannot both be the gospel." You must
have one or the other.

Let us look next at chart number ten. I am referring to
a debate that I attended shortly after I was baptized,
September, 1950. Here is the proposition: J. D. Holder
affirmed: "The Scriptures teach that all for whom Christ
died will be saved without the preached or written word or
any conditions on their part." He says, "My position is
[conditional on the part of Christ] . . . not . . . on the part of
the sinner." "Does the sinner work and secure salvation
by so doing? Elder Nichols," he says, "says yes . . . I say

Chart #9

Reference: Livingston Blauvelt, Jr., "Does the Bible Teach Lordship Salvation?" Bibliotheca Sacra 143:569 (January-March, 1986): 37-45.

"What is lordship salvation? This is the view that for salvation a person must trust Jesus Christ as his Savior from sin and must also commit himself to Christ as Lord of his life, submitting to His sovereign authority.

"This teaching is false because it subtly adds works to the clear and simple condition for salvation set forth in the Word of God. An unbeliever, to avail himself of the salvation offered in Christ, must only accept him as his own personal savior, believing that his death for sin was final and sufficient forever.

"According to the Bible, salvation is always by faith alone (Eph. 2:8-10). People can do nothing to merit God's gift of salvation, including making Jesus Christ Lord of their lives . . . To deny this truth is to deny man's total depravity and the sufficiency of Christ's death on the cross" (pp.37,38).

———

"However, justification is God's act of declaring a believer righteous at the moment he believes in Christ (Rom. 3:21-24; 5:1) (p.43).

———

"The question, Must one knowledgeably accept by faith Jesus as Lord (Sovereign Master) in order to be saved? has already be answered in the negative." (p.43).

———

"As Ryrie stated, 'The message of faith only and the message of faith plus commitment cannot both be the gospel; therefore one of them is false doctrine and comes under the curse of perverting the gospel or preaching another gospel (Gal. 1:6-9), and this is a very serious matter' " (p.44).

Quote from Charles C. Ryrie, Balancing the Christian Life (Chicago: Moody Press, 1969), p.170.

no!" "Is salvation . . . conditional?" He says it is "conditioned upon the work of God through Christ," and then it is applied to the sinner.

Now some quotations from within our brotherhood.

In July of 1991, brother Rubel Shelly, who later will speak today, made a speech on this subject in Jubilee 1991. There are several quotations that I have copied here, and I want to call attention to them with a full awareness that he is legitimately and properly entitled to explain what he says and what he means. [Chart #11.] It would rejoice my heart to understand that his words do not mean what they say. We shall see.

Chart #10

J. D. Holder
Primitive Baptist Debater
Milan, Tennessee (September 11-14, 1950)

Proposition:
"The Scriptures teach that all for whom Christ died will be saved or receive remission of sins without the preached or written word, or any conditions on their part."

Affirmed by J. D. Holder.

<u>Explanation:</u>
" . . . my position is, salvation through Christ, but not conditional on the part of the sinner."

"So the issue is: does the sinner work and secure salvation by so doing? Elder Nichols, as I understand his position, would say, 'Yes,' and I would say 'No.'

"Is salvation from the guilt of sins conditional? It is conditioned upon the work of God through Christ, his righteousness, and his obedience to the demands of the law, and then the application of it, in the work of salvation, giving the sinner the benefit of it, making him a child of God."

<u>Nichols-Holder Debate</u>, pages 20, 21.

I have the tape recorder from which I worked; I have the counter and a type script of some nineteen pages. Number one. Here is a quotation, page 2: "There is a righteousness God has given you through Christ, and your response there is not obedience to more commands, but faith."

A second quotation: "Our salvation arises entirely and only [there is that word *monon*, now] only from grace not by one thing that we bring, . . . not by one act, not by one deed, not by one righteous thing we do. It is entirely by grace through faith."

Does this allow for repentance as a condition? Well, we shall see.

In the next place, number three. "To teach baptism is the fifth step in the plan of salvation is a monstrosity. It's theologically horrible. It is not the fifth step. The one step to salvation is faith."

Next: "We are not the only fellowship of people that baptizes. We are not the only fellowship of people [watch this!] that admits people into the grace of God." What does that mean? I thought that God admitted us. Do we stand at the bar of entry and approve or not approve who can come in and receive the grace of God? Surely he does not mean that. And yet this is what he says. And then he states: "We do not admit folks. [Why the change?] Faith admits them."

And then next: "Baptism [he says] is not good because you got it all figured out, and you got all the theology parsed and you've got the sequencing right."

Notice that "sequencing." Does that mean that a person who says "I am saved by faith without baptism" is to be told, "Well, baptism is of no value anyway. The sequence between faith and baptism and salvation is not important." I do not believe he will say that, but I do believe this is what he said. We shall see.

Chart #11

QUOTATIONS FROM RUBEL SHELLY

"There's a righteousness God has given you through Christ. And your response there is not obedience to more commands, but faith."
Jubilee Speech, July 1991. [Counter 014, Typescript, p.2]

"Our salvation arises entirely and only from grace, not by one thing that we bring from this system over here, not by one act of duty, not by one deed of obedience, not by one righteous thing we do. It is entirely by grace through faith."
Jubilee Speech, July 1991. [Counter 264, Typescript, p.4]

"To teach baptism is the fifth step in the plan of salvation is a monstrosity. It's theologically horrible . . . It's not the fifth step. The one step to salvation is faith, but the faith that saves is not some mere mental assent."
Jubilee Speech, July 1991. [Counter 292, Typescript, pp.6,7]

"We're not the only fellowship of people that baptizes. We're not the only fellowship of people that admits people into the grace of God. We don't admit folks. Faith admits them."
Jubilee Speech, July 1991. [Counter 431, Typescript, p.12]

"Baptism is not good because you got it all figured out, and you got all the theology parsed, and you've got the sequencing right."
Jubilee Speech, July 1991. [Counter 451, Typescript, p.12]

"And, no, I'm not going to debate anybody on the theory whether salvation is by grace and grace alone; because the Bible just makes that too plain. In affirming that I do not deny human responsibility. Of course, we have responsibility. It's faith. But I'm saved after I have believed; I'm saved by what he did, not by my faith, and not by anything that in obedience to Christ I have done to demonstrate that my faith is genuine."
Jubilee Speech, July 1991. [Counter 766, Typescript, p.19]

He said: "No, I am not going to debate anyone on the theory whether salvation is by grace and grace alone, because the Bible just makes that too plain." He says there is "human responsibility." What is that responsibility? "It is faith." Is this faith alone? We shall see.

"But I am saved after I have believed; I am saved by what he did." Is this the echo of what J. D. Holder was saying in 1950? Perhaps we shall see. "Not by my faith." Wait a moment. Read that again. "We are saved," he says, "by grace alone." There is "human responsibility," but "I am saved" but "not by my faith, and not by anything that in obedience to Christ I have done to demonstrate that my faith is genuine." Is this what James was referring to in James 2:17,18—a dead faith?

Now another quotation, this time from the *Shelly-Moore Debate* in 1975. [Chart #12.] Notice the statement on page 116: "One does not trust the grace of God if he does not act in obedience to divine commandments." How can the statements made in 1975, in that debate, be reconciled with the statements I have just read? We shall see.

Let me turn now to introduce another aspect, this time from Robert Gundry. [Chart #13.] Gundry is wrestling with the same problem that we are going to wrestle with, and here is what he argues. He argues, and I appreciate the terminology: "For Paul, then, getting in [that is,

---

Chart #12

One does not trust the grace of God if he does not act in obedience to divine commands

—Jericho "given to Israel by God's grace [Joshua 6:16].
—Jericho received by Israel only "after" they walked around it for seven days [Heb. 11:30].

Shelly-Moore Debate, 1975, p.116

getting in Christ] and staying in Christ [notice "getting in, staying in," keep that terminology clear] are covered by the seamless robe of faith as opposed to works with the result that works come in as evidential rather than instrumental." Evidential? Yes. Instrumental? No. And he says the "bisection of getting in and staying in cuts the line through Paul's religion where the pattern shows a whole piece of cloth."

Now this runs him into a problem. And the problem is that if you have "the seamless robe of faith" and no works after you get in, what do you do with a sinner? Here is his answer: "The view that those professing Christians whose sin is so serious, prolonged, and unforsaken that they

---

Chart #13

ROBERT GUNDRY

<u>Reference:</u>

Robert Gundry, "Grace, Works and Staying Saved," <u>Biblica</u> **(1986): 1-38.**

<u>Getting In, Staying In</u>
<u>Evidential Works? Instrumental Works?</u>

"For Paul, then, getting in and staying in are covered by the seamless robe of faith as opposed to works, with the result that works come in as evidential rather than instrumental. Sanders' [E. P., ww] bisection of getting in and staying in cuts a line through Paul's religion where the pattern shows a whole piece of cloth" (p.12).

<u>Serious, Prolonged, Unforsaken Sin</u>

"Therefore, the view that those professing Christians whose sin is so serious, prolonged, and unforsaken that they apparently lose their salvation never really had it in the first place looks to be a fair extrapolation from Paul's thinking." (Page 22, Footnote 25).

Chart #14
EPHESIANS 2:8-10

"For by grace are ye saved through faith" (KJV)
"For by grace have ye been saved through faith" (ASV)
"For by grace you have been saved through faith" (RSV)
"For it is by grace that you have been saved, through faith"
(NIV)

———————— ἐστε σεσωσμένοι ————————

"Getting In"

1. Reference to this only?
2. Does "by faith" exclude "works" of which one can boast?
3. Does "by faith" exclude obedience to the gospel?
   (a) Repentance?
   (b) Confession?
   (c) Baptism to be saved? (Mk .16:16)
4. Does "grace" exclude obedience to the gospel?
   (a) Repentance?
   (b) Confession?
   (c) Baptism to be saved? (Mk. 16:16)
5. Are repentance, confession, and baptism:
   (a) Evidential only?
   (b) Instrumental only?
   (c) Evidential and Instrumental?
6. Are repentance, confession, and baptism "works of the law" (Gal. 3:10)?
7. Does obedience to the gospel equal obeying, doing the law of Moses?

"Staying In"

1. Reference to this only?
2. Does "by faith" exclude "works" of which one can boast?
3. Does "by faith" exclude "good works" God has ordained?
4. Does "grace" exclude "good works" God ordained?
5. Are "good works":
   (a) Evidential only?
   (b) Instrumental only?
   (c) Evidential and instrumental?
6. Are the "good works" of Eph. 2:10 "works of the law" (Gal. 3:10)?
7. Does doing the "good works" here equal doing, obeying the law of Moses?

apparently lose their salvation never really had it in the first place looks to be a fair extrapolation from Paul's teaching." Now this gets to the heart of what I now want to talk about in some depth.

I call attention to chart number 14. Notice the same verses, but particularly the words *este sesosmenoi*. *Este sesosmenoi*, hold that in your mind for a moment and turn please, to chart number 15 and then we will come back to that. Notice in chart number 15: "*Este sesosmenoi*." This is a perfect passive periphrastic indicative of *sodzo*. Greek students will grasp the point. Those who also may not read Greek will grasp what C. D. F. Moule says. Notice his statement concerning this periphrastic in Ephesians 2:8. "As a result of free favor you are saved, but nevertheless you have been saved and therefore enjoy your present status." This is exactly where I appreciated what brother Oster was saying. He laid the ground work for my discussion right here and I thank him. We did not compare notes; we have not talked or written or sent communication. I believe the harmony is a result of reading the same book, not collusion.

Notice the words of James H. Moulton here, very important concerning the periphrastic in Ephesians 2:5,8 "of a work which is finished on its Author's side but progressively realized by its objects," exactly what Rick was saying.

The reference is to "getting in" or "staying in." My questions—and I believe these need to be addressed as the evening proceeds—are, is the statement of "saved by grace through faith" a reference to "getting in" only? Is it a reference to "staying in" only? I maintain it is both, because *este sesosmenoi* combines the past and the ongoingness of their salvation. We shall see as we move further.

Number two. Does "by faith" in reference to "getting in" exclude works of which one can boast? I would say,

Chart #15

Gus Nichols, <u>Sermons by Gus Nichols and Others</u>
(1949).
<u>Divine Side of Salvation</u>
Page 62, 63:

"On the divine side of the plan of salvation all is done for man by grace. It was by the grace of God that Christ came to seek and to save the lost. (2 Cor. 8:9; Lk. 19:10.) . . . Then after the sinner obeys the gospel, God by grace pardons and forgives the sinner and makes him his child and a member of his church. This is all done by grace (Eph. 2:4-5). Hence, man obeys and God saves."

Two Sides of Salvation
<u>Grace and Faith</u>
Page 63:

"The two sides of the plan of salvation are represented by grace and faith. All God does for our salvation is done by grace, while all man does in order to be saved by grace must be done through faith."

<u>"Saving" Grace an "Active" Grace</u>
Page 64:

"Grace is a broad term, and includes all that God has done for our salvation - his love, the gift of his Son, the death of Christ, and finally pardon itself. Every act of his was an act of grace. We are saved by grace which did something - and not by a dead inactive grace. By grace God DID WONDERFUL THINGS FOR US. Prompted by grace he DID ALL THINGS which we could not do for ourselves."

<u>"Saving" Faith an Active Faith</u>
Page 64

"Likewise, we must do something to be saved by faith. Prompted by faith, we must obey the gospel and,

Chart #15, cont'd

thus, accept the salvation grace provided, at such awful cost. Just as God did all he did for us prompted by his grace and mercy, we must take every step in obeying the gospel by faith . . . Each requirement of God is a step of faith (Rom. 4:12). Repentance, confession and baptism are only steps of faith. Acceptable obedience to the gospel is faith exercised unto salvation. Instead of being saved by a dead faith, our faith must be put into action, or be expressed in obedience to God before it saves" (Heb. 5:8,9; 1 Pet. 1:22; Mk. 16:16; Acts 2:38).

God's Part; Man's Part In Salvation
Page 64

"Hence, the sinner by faith does what God says he must do to be saved, and then God does the saving, and does it by his wonderful favor and grace."

yes. Does "staying in" by faith exclude works of which one can boast? My answer is, yes.

Number three. Does "by faith" exclude obedience to the gospel? My answer, no. Does "by faith" exclude good works God has ordained. My answer, no.

Number four. What about "getting in." Does grace with reference to "getting in" exclude obedience to the gospel? Does it exclude repentance? Does it exclude confession? Does it exclude baptism to be saved? This is the heartbeat of the discussion. Does "grace" exclude "good works" God has ordained? Now, are repentance, confession, and baptism "evidential only," just a fruit of faith, in no way connected with being saved? Are they "only instrumental," in no way connected with faith but effective in and of themselves apart from faith? I would maintain they are both "evidential" and "instrumental." What about "good works"? Are they "evidential only"? Are they

---

Chart #16

ROBERT L. SAUCY <u>Reference</u>: Robert L. Saucy, "Second Response to 'Faith According to the Apostle James' by John F. MacArthur, Jr.," JETS 33/11 (March 1990): 43-47.

TYPICAL VIEW OF DENOMINATIONAL WORLD CONCERNING FAITH AND WORKS

Page 44:
"Traditional interpretation of the notion of 'faith' and 'works' in James never attempted to merge James' 'works' together with 'faith' so that the 'works' are a part of justifying faith. Rather, they have been careful to distinguish them, making faith alone the justifying cause and works the inevitable fruit of a genuine living faith."

"WORKS" GIVE EVIDENCE THAT "FAITH" IS "ALIVE"

Page 44:
"As spirit in a body gives evidence that the body is alive, so works give evidence that faith is alive. To phrase it differently: If the body gives no evidence of spirit or the life principle it is judged dead. Likewise faith if it gives no evidence of works it is dead."

NATURE OF FAITH AND WAYS OF SALVATION

Page 45:
"But the nature of faith required [of the woman at the well and the rich young ruler] obviously was the same in each instance, for there cannot be different ways of salvation."

"WORKS" THE FRUIT OF "SAVING FAITH"

Page 46,47:
"As in nature, there is clearly some connection between the root or seed and the plant or fruit that grows on it. If some kind of obedience represented by the works of James is necessarily the fruit of saving faith, then it is difficult to see how some dimension of obedience can be totally excluded from the seed of faith."

Chart #16, cont'd

**"JUSTIFYING FAITH" AND "SANCTIFYING FAITH"
DIFFERENT IN ESSENCE?**

Page 47:
"Another way of looking at the issue is to ask whether
the nature of justifying faith is essentially different from
the nature of sanctifying faith assuming that sanctification is really by faith even as is the case with justification.
Now it seems clear that some element of a will oriented
toward obedience is involved in the very essence of
sanctifying faith, if, in fact, such faith produces obedience. Unless we are prepared to say that this is a totally
new element added to the nature of sanctifying faith that
was not present in any aspect in the saving or justifying
faith, it would seem that we have to acknowledge some
aspect of obedience inherent in saving faith as well."

"instrumental only"? No, they are both "evidential" and
"instrumental."

Question: Are repentance, confession, and baptism
works of the law in Galatians 3:10? I would say, no. We
shall see what others say. Are the good works of Ephesians
2:10 the works of the law? No. Does obedience to the
gospel equal obeying or doing the law of Moses? No. Does
doing the good works equal doing or obeying the Old
Testament law? The answer is, no.

Quickly now to chart number 15. I read again recently
the words of the man who baptized me into Christ, one of
God's greatest noblemen. I never in this world expect to
see another man to equal him. In the year 1949, he wrote
these words in the heat of sustained discussion of the plan
of salvation among the Baptist people of my beloved Walker
County. Listen to his words:

> On the divine side of the plan of salvation, all is done for
> man by grace. It was by the grace of God that Christ came

to seek and save the lost . . . Then after the sinner obeys the gospel, God by grace pardons and forgives the sinner and makes him his child and a member of his church. This is all done by grace . . . The two sides of the plan of salvation are represented by grace and faith. All God does for our salvation is done by grace, while all man does in order to be saved by grace must be done through faith. Grace is a broad term and includes all that God has done for our salvation—his love, the gift of his Son. Every act of his was an act of grace. We are saved by grace which did something, not by a dead inactive grace. By grace God DID WONDERFUL THINGS FOR US. Prompted by grace, he DID ALL THINGS which we could not do for ourselves . . . Likewise we must do something to be saved by faith. Prompted by faith, we must obey the gospel and, thus accept the salvation grace provided at such awful cost. Just as God did all he did for us prompted by his grace and mercy, we must take every step in obeying the gospel by faith . . . Each requirement of God is a step of faith. Repentance, confession, and baptism are only steps of faith. Acceptable obedience to the gospel is faith exercised unto salvation. Instead of being saved by a dead faith, our faith must be put into action.

Is this a faith that does not "demonstrate its genuineness"? I say, no. We shall see what others say. It must be "expressed" in obedience to God before it saves . . . "Hence, the sinner by faith does what God says he must do to be saved, and then God does the saving and does it by his wonderful favor and grace."

[Chart #16.] Notice next Robert Saucy. Saucy is wrestling with a problem of Lordship salvation. He operates out of a denominational background I would not share; but nevertheless, he is wrestling with the problem of faith and works and James 2. That comes in this afternoon but it is pertinent here. Notice on page 44:

As spirit in a body gives evidence that the body is alive, so works give evidence that faith is alive. To phrase it differently: If the body gives no evidence of spirit or the life principle it is judged dead. Likewise faith if it is gives no evidence of works it is dead.

Someone told us that "I am saved by faith, but it is not one that demonstrates its genuineness by anything I've done." We shall see as the day goes on.

Page 45: "The nature of the faith required [of the woman at the well and the rich young ruler] obviously was the same in each instance, for there cannot be different ways of salvation."

And then finally, on page 46 and 47:

> As in nature, there is clearly some connection between the root or seed and the plant or fruit that grows it. If some kind of obedience represented by the works of James is necessarily the fruit of saving faith, then it is difficult to see how some dimension of obedience can be totally excluded from the seed of faith.

And his last quotation, page 47. This comes up in reference to justifying, sanctifying faith—now the Bible does not use that terminology. That is man's language. You can not read "justifying faith" and "saving faith" and "sanctifying faith" in the Bible to save your life. If so, where is it? But using his terminology:

> Another way of looking at the issue is to ask whether the nature of justifying faith is essentially different [*essentially different*] from the nature of sanctifying faith assuming that sanctification is really by faith even as is the case with justification. Now it seems clear that some element of a will oriented to obedience is involved in the very essence of sanctifying faith [his terminology] if, in fact, such faith produces obedience. Unless we are prepared [we are back to *sesosmenoi* now, back to *dia*]— Unless we are prepared to say that this is a totally new element added to the nature of sanctifying faith that was not present in any aspect in the saving or justifying faith, it would seem that we have to acknowledge some aspect of obedience inherent in saving faith as well.

Quickly now in closing. I ask brother Shelly in his remarks later in the day, to please, in light of this discussion, explain his statement in *Arbeit Macht Frei!*: "It is a scandalous and outrageous lie to teach that salvation arises from human activity." We will discuss, I presume, the meaning of the word *arises*. I have come prepared to discuss it to the best of my ability. "We do not contribute one whit to our salvation." I plan to discuss *contribute* as need be. "*Arbeit Macht Frei!* is the falsehood against which both Romans and Galatians protest." Romans and Galatians do not protest the divine side of salvation. They protest the Jewish, Judaistic effort to add the works of the law of Moses of a selected nature to the way of salvation. We will discuss that later on in light of C. D. F. Moule and other matters of importance.

My time is gone and I appreciate your attention.

Rubel Shelley

Rubel Shelly has served as minister at Woodmont Hills Church of Christ in Nashville since 1978. Concurrently he has served as Adjunct Assistant Professor in the Department of Medicine (Medical Ethics) at Vanderbilt (1986-1988); assistant Professor of Philosophy at David Lipscomb University (1981-1983); and Graduate Assistant in the Department of Philosophy at Vanderbilt (1979-1980). Prior to his moving to Nashville, he served as an instructor at Freed-Hardeman University in the Department of Religion and Philosophy (1975-1979).

He received the B.A. degree at Harding University (1968); the M.A. and M.Th. from Harding Graduate School of Religion (1972, 1976); and the M.A. and Ph.D. from Vanderbilt University (1980, 1981).

Rubel and Myra Shappley Shelly have three children: Myra Michelle Arms, Timothy James, and Thomas Rubel, Jr.

Writings include *The Art of being Married, Young People and Their Lord, In Step With the Spirit, Prepare to Answer*, and *Things That Last.* Many professional and popular-level articles have appeared in journals, magazines, and newspapers.

Rubel holds membership in the American Philosophical Association and the Christian Medical Society.

Grace and Works in Romans 4-5 and James 2:14-26

Rubel Shelly

In my attempt to make a contribution to our time together, I wish to proceed in three moves. First, I will articulate the theology of salvation I believe and teach from the New Testament. Second, I will offer an exposition of Romans 4 and, third, of James 2:14-26 as primary texts to which one would appeal to legitimate that theology. Then I will close with some personal observations about the theme.

The bad news is written both on the pages of Scripture and human history: No one can live a life so pleasing to God that he or she will be declared righteous in his sight. "Therefore no one will be declared righteous in his sight by observing the law . . . for all have sinned and fall short of the glory of God" (Rom. 3:20a, 23).

The Good News is written on the billboard that is the cross of Jesus Christ: All those who trust God's work on their behalf will be judged righteous in him. "But now a righteousness from God, apart from law, has been made known . . . This righteousness comes through faith in Jesus Christ to all who believe" (Rom. 3:21,22).

Have you heard the story of the judge whose son appeared before him on a drunk-driving charge? Because he was sworn to uphold justice, the man behind the bench had to find him guilty; then he imposed the heaviest fine allowed under the law. But he immediately stepped down from his chair and paid the fine from his own pocket.

That is a tiny glimpse of what God has done for us. Unable to declare us innocent under the law and knowing we could not set right the wrongs we had done, he pronounced us "Guilty!" and imposed the law's full penalty—death. Then Jesus Christ went to the cross and paid the penalty for us.

So what is left for us to do to establish the basis for righteousness before God? Nothing. Absolutely nothing! If there were anything for us to add, salvation would not be God's work. If we contributed anything at all to our justification as sinners, the glory for salvation would not be God's alone. The blood of Christ has paid for our redemption *in full*, and we do not even pay the sales tax on the purchase! Salvation arises from the grace of God, not at the end of our attainments or on the basis of our ability to obey law, accumulate "brownie points," or otherwise prove ourselves "worthy" of salvation. To teach that redemption is grounded in human wisdom or performance is false doctrine of the most unworthy sort.

Yet there are *requirements* we must meet in order to accept the free, undeserved, and unmerited gift offered in Christ. Our "access . . . into this grace in which we now stand" is "by faith" (Rom. 5:2a). This access-faith is more than the mental assent that demons—on some points, at least—give to certain tenets of Christian theology (Jas. 2:19). Access to grace is by a faith that is submissive and obedient, for "faith without deeds is dead" (Jas. 2:26).

This faith that I have just characterized as "submissive and obedient" is not, however, an element of legalistic theology that holds the cross to be "God's part" of redemption and obedience to divine commandments "man's part." It is instead a biblical theology that proclaims God's work at the cross as the sum total of meritorious activity associated with salvation and that our obedient faith is nothing more than open-handed acceptance of the free gift purchased by the blood of Christ. The grace of God will not be forced on unwilling recipients. Thus the entailments of faith are not "options" to our salvation; they are essentials.

First, we must see ourselves as we really are. That is, we must accept the judgment of God against humankind that we are guilty of sin, justly condemned under divine law, and unable to set right our broken relationship with God. Remember the parable of the two men praying at the temple? (Luke 18:9-14). Only one of them went home justified that day.

Second, we must be willing to abandon the deeds—and their underlying attitudes—that have set us against God. We must turn away from sin, for it is absurd to expect God to forgive things we intend to keep doing. The biblical term for this requirement is "repentance." Since old habits die hard, repentance is best thought of as a *willingness* to abandon sin rather than a one-time spiritual occurrence. Anyone following Jesus must "deny himself and take up his cross *daily*" (Lk. 9:23).

Third, having given up on self-justification and self-righteousness, we turn for salvation to the "righteousness from God [that] comes through faith in Jesus Christ to all who believe." That we have died to self so as to live in Christ is symbolized in baptism—the reenactment of the death, burial, and resurrection of Jesus Christ. Though a symbol of a greater reality, baptism is no *mere* symbol. It is

essential to the objective reality of a sinner's turn from
darkness to light, from death to life, from judgment to
redemption (Rom. 6:3,4).

The God of grace makes sinners righteous in Christ
Jesus. With nothing in our hands to bring, we are saved on
condition of trust in him (i.e., faith) that shows itself in
genuine repentance and Christ-affirming baptism (Acts
2:36-38). Thus has our God been both *just* in honoring the
condemnation of sinners under the stipulations of law and
the *Justifier* of all who would trust his method of paying
the penalty sin required. For a work so great that only God
could achieve it, we must praise him as Savior and give him
all the glory. We must abandon our pretenses, swallow our
pride, and trust him for the right standing we want but
cannot attain by our flawed obedience to law.

Romans is Paul's deliberate and thoughtful examina-
tion of the gospel. The heart of the epistle is 1:18-8:39. The
entire section might be headed "Justification By Faith"
and divided the following way: The universal *need* for
salvation (1:18-3:20), the *source* of salvation in the redemptive work of Christ (3:21-26), the *reception* of salvation
(3:27-4:25), and the *results* of salvation (5:1-8:39).

Although the whole world—pagan, moralist, and
Jew—is in need of redemption, no one can be saved by
keeping law. "What law?" someone asks. Any law. Law of
Moses, Code of Hammurabi, gospel preached as a law code,
or law written on the heart—nobody will be justified by a
system of law-keeping. Justification by law-keeping demands perfect compliance with law, and no one will ever be
justified by this means. Paul affirms: "But now a righteousness from God, apart from law, has been made known,
to which the Law and the Prophets testify. This righteousness from God comes through faith in Jesus Christ to all
who believe" (Rom. 3:21-22a).

There are at least three critical moves in this statement. First is the use of the word *righteousness*

(*dikaiosune*). It may have either of two meanings in Scripture when used in relation to human beings. It sometimes stands for an ethical concept which denotes virtue, integrity, and upright conduct. At other times, it is used as a soteriological concept to denote a status of rightness, freedom from sin, right standing before God. When used as an ethical concept, righteousness is something to be performed or carried out in one's life; it has to do with conduct. Used as a soteriological concept, however, the word has nothing to do with what humans accomplish by our effort. It has not to do with performance but position. It is a status of right standing with God that is bestowed on people as a free gift from God. It is undeserved and unearned. It is God's act of accepting ungodly persons as if they were godly.

Second, the apostle's statement is that the righteousness of God is "apart from law." Right-standing with God cannot come by fulfilling the requirements of law, for we are not and never have been successful law-keepers. Oh, we do better on some days than on others and with some commandments than with others. But since law is a single fabric, "whoever keeps the whole law and yet stumbles at just one point is guilty of breaking it all" (Jas. 2:10). If any one among us is saved, then, it will have to be by some means other than keeping law.

Third, the righteousness of God that cannot come to us through law comes instead "through faith in Jesus Christ to all who believe." When one realizes he is a sinner and lost, he can either try to be righteous in his own strength through law-keeping and good works or accept the fact that all his attempts at setting things right with God are doomed to failure and trust God to offer us something we cannot deserve. Thus the affirmation of Paul is constantly to the effect that salvation is not by our good works but is only and always by faith. Yet the faith that saves is never dead or disobedient faith. It is the faith of submission and obedience already characterized in this presentation.

Paul knew it would be difficult for some of his original readers to accept the doctrine of justification by grace through faith. This would be so especially for Jews who had come to trust in their law-keeping. Like the Pharisee praying with the tax collector, some of them liked to remind God and one another of their committed obedience and personal piety. Knowing that a picture is worth a thousand words, the apostle chose to put the issue to a test case. If Abraham was justified by his works under law, Paul's opponents were correct; if he was justified instead by faith, Paul was right (Rom. 4:1-3).

Abraham's case related to two points Paul had made in Romans 3. First, those who had lived even before Christ's day served God acceptably through faith rather than by perfect rule-keeping. Second, faith upholds divine law rather than repudiates it. Referring back to Genesis 15, Paul reminded his readers of God's promise of a great reward for Abraham. Yet Abraham complained that he was childless and without an heir to perpetuate his line. Yahweh brought the patriarch outside his tent, told him to look toward heaven, and said that his descendants would be as numerous as the stars of heaven. The Bible says: "Abram believed the Lord, and he credited it to him as righteousness" (Gen. 15:6).

In spite of the unlikeliness of this promise being fulfilled, Abraham trusted God for its legitimation. At times his faith grew weak and was compromised by sinful actions on his part (for example, the Ishmael episode, Genesis 16). But his faith was properly placed in God, and God vindicated his faith by giving him the promised son, Isaac. It was neither Abraham's understanding of biology nor his upright behavior that produced the fulfillment of the promise. It was God's knowledge and activity that brought about a happy conclusion. Abraham's faith in that divine power is what justified him in that episode. Had it been otherwise, he would have been justified by works and would have received his reward as the payment of a divine debt to him (Rom. 4:4-5).

It reminds me of an episode in my own life from 25 years ago. My father knew about my need for a new car. He knew the automobile I wanted and arranged with the man who owned a certain dealership for me to have it. He told me to go to the dealer, deliver my car, put an envelope he gave me in the dealer's hand, and pick up the one he knew I had been wanting. I believed him that the arrangements were made and acted on that faith by traveling 16 miles, finding the dealer, giving him the envelope, and claiming by faith what he had promised me. I didn't drive that new car home and boast to people of my ability to work hard, save money, and buy nice things. My boasting was—and continues to be—about the generosity of my father. It was by grace through faith and not of myself. That is the same way our dealings with God go.

Going further, Paul insists that God not only credits righteousness to sinners by faith but also declines to charge further sin to believers he has thus justified (Rom. 4:6-8). "The man whose sin the Lord will never count against him" is the same person John later described at 1 John 1:7. He is not the perfect man whose righteousness is that of performance (cf. 1 John 1:8, 10); it is the sinful man who walks in the light of faith and continually acknowledges his sinfulness (cf. 1 John 1:9).

The forgiveness we receive by the blood of Christ is not merely for sins of the past but for all time to come. Until a believer repudiates his or her salvation by a conscious decision to "deliberately keep on sinning after we have received the knowledge of the truth" (Heb. 10:26), he or she is secure in Christ. Even when we "mess up," we are still safe in the love and grace of God. We don't have to be spiritual neurotics who wonder from one minute to the next about our salvation, for we are those persons the Lord will never charge with sin.

Art Buchwald discussed the Yiddish word *chutzpa* in one of his newspaper columns. He said it has no English equivalent but refers to one who has an attitude of incredible gall or presumption. "The classic case of a chutzpa," he says, "is the young man who murders his parents and then asks the court to show mercy because he is an orphan." The arrogant person who sins presumptuously will fall from grace, but the still-struggling, still-weak, and still-sinning believer need have no fear. Both his original access into Christ and his security in him are by grace.

At this juncture in his argument, Paul makes a point that would offend many Jews. He reminds his readers of the chronology of Abraham's justification. Abraham himself was still uncircumcised when the things just narrated happened (Rom. 4:9-11a). This means that he is "the father of all who believe" (Rom. 4:11b). This is an elaboration on Romans 3:29 and drives home the point that all who follow Abraham's example, whether Jew or Gentile, are heirs to the justification that comes by faith (Rom. 4:12,13).

The next three verses contain a line of argument that is difficult for us to follow. Many have interpreted them apart from their larger context and have missed the apostle's point. They are best understood as a recapitulation of the entire section begun at Romans 3:27. Law, works, and merit stand together on one side; grace, faith, and promise stand together on the other side. Anyone who chooses to stand on the side of the former stands under condemnation, for one seeking divine favor through performance cannot but fail. Where there is law there is transgression, and where there is transgression there is wrath (Rom.

4:14,15a). Only where there is no law can there be no transgression with its accompanying wrath (4:15b). That one place of security is found by those who stand on the side of grace, faith, and promise. One becomes an heir through faith in the divine promise when he or she, following the steps of Abraham, trusts God's process of redemption rather than human counterfeits. Whether Jew or Gentile, all those who are true believers in God trace their spiritual lineage to Abraham, "the father of us all" (Rom. 4:16,17a).

The character of Abraham's faith is Paul's topic in the next six verses. Two ideas are essential to our discussion.

First, Abraham's faith was fixed on the right object. He did not trust himself, his ability to fathom mysteries, or his ability to see how things could work out as God has promised. He put his trust entirely in God and his ability to fulfill his word. He believed in a God who could give life to the dead and summon nonexisting things into being (Rom. 4:17b), who could justify hoping for an end that all human hope had already abandoned (Rom. 4:18), and who could cause two people well beyond child-bearing age to have a child of promise (Rom. 4:19). It was this attitude toward God's faithfulness that was "credited to him as righteousness" (Rom. 4:20-22).

Second, Abraham's faith is held up as the model for Christian faith. The story of his trust in God is not in the Bible simply as a tribute to the patriarch (Rom. 4:23). It is there also for us to encourage us to pattern our faith after his (Rom. 4:23,24a). Specifically, we are called to "believe in him who raised Jesus our Lord from the dead" (Rom. 4:24b). Abraham's God and the one who raised Jesus from the dead are not different deities; in the latter, however, is a more fully revealed God who has shown his face in human form. We are called to believe that God acted through Jesus Christ who was "delivered over to death for our sins and was raised to life for our justification" (Rom. 4:25). It was not the death alone but the resurrection that followed on which we base the assurance of faith. We know he is the Son of God and only Savior by virtue of heaven's action in raising him from the dead with power and thereby vindicating all the fantastic claims he made for himself.

I suppose one would need no more justification for moving directly from Romans 4 to James 2 than that Abraham is central to both texts as a case study for the nature of faith. What it says on the topic of faith and deeds is certainly important to the study at hand.

James opens with the clear affirmation that faith apart from action is dead (Jas. 2:16,17). His Spirit-guided illustration of this truth concerns a brother who is destitute and hungry. One sees this brother's needs and says, "Good luck to you!" How much good has he done the man? Should he not have backed up his profession of good will with some tangible relief? James is here underscoring again the theme of this whole epistle—Christianity must be practical in order to be real. Actions are necessary to validate faith.

James moves next to anticipate a possible objection. Someone might say, "But different people may choose to exhibit their religion in different ways—one by faith and another by deeds." He challenges anyone who would make so naive a statement to show his faith apart from the fruit it produces in his life (Jas. 2:18-20).

There is no proof that a man has faith at all unless some fruit is borne of it in his life. Even the demons believe in the one true God; but they are lost and doomed forever because they did not, in their previous existence as angels (cf. 2 Pet. 2:4), submit to God's authority. The same sad fate will befall the *chutzpa* who professes faith yet lives in rebellion against God's will.

Two familiar and clear examples of faith that saves are set forth in the text. First, he raises the classic case of

Abraham (Jas. 2:21-24). The Jewish Christians who first read this epistle would be familiar with the fact that Abraham was the "father of the faithful" or the "father of those who believe." Yet James reminds his readers that Abraham was justified when, by faith, he offered Isaac as a sacrifice (cf. Gen. 22:1-19; Heb. 11:17-19). Second, there is the case of Rahab (Jas. 2:25). This example of faith takes the reader back to the time of Israel's entry into Canaan. Joshua sent spies into Jericho to bring back a report concerning that city. The faith of Rahab that these men were from God would have been in vain if she had not acted on her conviction. She did act by hiding the men and later sending them out safely to join the Israelites. Shortly thereafter, when her home city of Jericho was given to God's people in a terrible battle, Rahab and her family were spared destruction because of her faith (Josh. 2:1-24).

The only legitimate conclusion to be drawn from these examples is this: One is saved by his faith when that faith lives and produces submission to God. Faith that refuses to obey is not saving faith. As Bonhoeffer said: "Only those who obey can believe, and only those who believe can obey." One does not truly believe God if he is not willing to follow God's directions. "As the body without the spirit is dead, so faith without deeds is dead" (Jas. 2:26).

What shall we make of the contradiction that some say exists between the teaching of James and Paul on this subject? If one understands that these two men are writing to different audiences and dealing with altogether different matters, the suspicion of contradiction vanishes.

Paul was writing to refute certain false teachers who taught that salvation depended on doing good works and accumulating merit for them. For some, those meritorious deeds would have been the works of the Law of Moses. Thus they would have attempted to bind circumcision, sabbath-keeping and certain other Old Testament ordinances on New Testament Christians. Paul asserted that the works of the Law have nothing to do with the salvation of men under the authority of Christ. More than that, no amount of rule-keeping under any system—pagan, Jewish, or Christian—can remedy a sinner's relationship with God.

On the other hand, James was writing to refute the false notion that faith—understood as inner conviction and personal confidence—was all that mattered in religion. He taught that inner conviction has to show itself in the outward deeds of the individual. Thus it is that the "contradiction" in these two passages is only imagined rather than real. Paul and James were discussing two different types of works. Paul's interest was more in the soteriological understanding of righteousness, and James was concerned in his epistle with the ethical demands of righteousness. Thus the former emphasized grace as the ground and basis of salvation, and the latter stressed good works as the outgrowth of salvation.

Just as surely as there are two types of faith discussed in the New Testament (dead faith and living faith), so are two types of works discussed (deeds of meritorious good works and what I earlier called the deeds of submissive and obedient faith).

Paul and James are in perfect harmony in their teaching on this matter. Both make it clear that faith and obedience are not in opposition to each other. They are two sides of the same coin in God's plan for the salvation of man. Man must believe in God and take him at his word. Based on that faith, he must set his heart to obey the commands God has given. At the end of all he has done, however, he gives God praise for saving him by grace; he makes no claim to be saved by his own good deeds.

To say it another way, there is only one "because of" to the plan of salvation. God's love as shown at the cross is the one and only ground of redemption. Thus we are not saved because we pray, give money to good causes, stop beating our wives, get sober, take the Lord's supper, get baptized, or attend church regularly. Actions such as the ones listed above are appropriate—and even, in some cases, essential—deeds for one who is approaching God by faith. But, even if one does everything he is commanded to do and follows every life instruction appropriate to faith, he is still an "unprofitable servant" who has merely done his duty and must give all the glory for his salvation to God alone (Luke 17:7-10). And if he uses these commandments and instructions as a legalistic means into God's favor or teaches others the gospel as a legalism, he comes under the anathema of God and falls from grace (Gal. 1:6-9; 5:4).

In a nutshell, the biblical tension is never between faith and action. It is between faith and merit as the ground of one's salvation.

To the non-Christian, this means that he cannot afford to fall prey to the false denominational doctrine of salvation by faith alone. One cannot be saved from his sins by simply "trusting Christ as your personal Savior and receiving him into your heart." This doctrine dates back to a wrong turn in Reformation theology and contradicts the clear teaching of James 2:24 and other New Testament passages. Inquiring sinners of the first century were not told, "Only believe and do nothing more!" They were commanded, "Repent and be baptized, every one of you, in the name of Jesus Christ for the forgiveness of your sins. And you will receive the gift of the Holy Spirit" (Acts 2:38).

To the Christian, this means that his life must bear fruit daily if he is to demonstrate his new state in the Lord and avoid falling away. His faith must prompt him to faithfulness in spiritual things. Otherwise his faith is dead and utterly without value.

Salvation rests upon and arises from the grace of God. We don't deserve it. We can't be worthy of it. It will always

be a free gift. Yet it remains the case that not everyone
who is offered the free gift will be saved, for some remain in
unbelief. Faith as trust, submission, and obedience to God
is the means of access into grace. Then, justified by grace
through faith, our lives are given over to the pursuit of
good works that give God glory. These good works are
"Thank Yous" from redeemed people and contribute nothing to the ground of our salvation. They are rather the
natural outcome of a redemptive work that is being done in
our hearts by the indwelling Spirit of God. As he lives
within us, our lives bear the lovely fruit that testifies to his
presence.

Though we could never have devised so grand a scheme
of redemption, we may have its benefits freely in Christ. As
with Abraham and Rahab, so with us: Not because we
have worked for it but because we have trusted God's work
on our behalf, we are credited with a *status* of righteousness (right-standing) with him and strive daily for the
demonstration of righteousness (God-honoring behavior).
There is no room at any point in this process for boasting.
We can only praise God for his grace.

As we preach the gospel then, let us preach it faithfully
as the message of the grace of God. Lest we be heard as
preaching a legalistic message, let us put the emphasis on
what God has done to provide redemption rather than on
what we must do to receive it. Such an approach is faithful
to the pattern of Pentecost. The sermon that day was not
titled "Repent and Be Baptized!" but "Jesus is Lord and
Christ!" When Christ was exalted, hearers asked the
question about their responsibility and were told about
repentance and baptism. I have found that the same
method of preaching produces the same inquiring response.

A five-night gospel meeting with "Hear," "Believe,"
"Repent," "Confess Christ," and "Be Baptized" as topics
doesn't look very much like the preaching pattern in Acts.
It generates an issue-oriented series of confrontations and

seldom results in anyone other than our own children (and increasingly few of them) being "converted." On the other hand, preaching that lifts up Jesus, explains the meaning of the cross, and focuses on the greatness of the love and mercy of God toward sinners attracts broken people, gives them hope for healing, and moves them to ask what they need to do to experience redeeming grace.

I like the story of a man who was telling of his deliverance from a life of sin. He gave God all the glory, saying nothing about what he had put away or learned to do. A rather legalistic brother had listened as long as he could and said, "You seem to indicate that God did everything when he saved you. Didn't you have to do your part before God did his?" "Oh, yes," said the new Christian. "For more than 30 years I ran away from God as fast as my sins could carry me. That was *my part*, but God took out after me and ran me down at the cross. That was *his part.*"

Fruitful good works done in obedience to God are the constant goal of Christian living. They are neither the foundation of our relationship with God nor the basis on which we will stand before him justified in the Last Day. Our confidence rests on his grace witnessed most perfectly at the cross of Christ. Those men and women everywhere who have accepted the free gift of salvation through a living faith that has confessed and claimed the death, burial, and resurrection of Christ in believer's baptism have had Christ's own righteousness credited to our account. We are justified not on the basis of our performance but because of his great redemptive sacrifice. Weak, struggling, and sinful still, we rejoice in "him who is able to keep you from falling and to present you before his glorious presence without fault and with great joy" (Jude 24).

> My sin, O the bliss of this glorious thought,
> My sin, not in part, but the whole,
> Is nailed to the cross, and I bear it no more:
> Praise the Lord, praise the Lord, O my soul!

Keith A. Mosher, Sr.

Keith Mosher presently serves as Dean of Academics at Memphis School of Preaching where he was graduated in 1975 and has worked since 1984.

He was graduated summa cum laude from Southern Christian University in 1984. He holds the B.A., M.A. and M.Th. degrees from that university. In May of 1992, Harding Graduate School of Religion conferred a D.Min. degree upon him.

Mission work includes gospel meetings in Australia and Africa. He has served churches in Mississippi, Tennessee, Pennsylvania, and Indiana.

Religious articles have appeared in *The Spiritual Sword*, *Power*, *Gospel Advocate*, *Bible Light*, and other publications. He has written three books and numerous lectureship articles.

Keith is married to Dorothy Carol. The Moshers have three children and five grandchildren. Their first grandchild (James) died at the age of five months.

Grace and Works in Romans 4-5 and James 2:14-26

Keith Mosher

It is good to be here today and to have this small part in discussing a most vital subject.

I commend the graduate school for this forum and especially the alumni association. It has a pertinent subject; it is been well discussed today already. Some teaching often causes resistance and discord among us, but we are grateful to be here today to discuss the subject of God's grace, law, faith, and works.

Some of the things I hear from time to time are what I heard when I was in the Presbyterian Church before 1965. And I think sometimes when we are trying to emphasize certain aspects of this subject we may tend to overemphasize some things. And in the brief discussions, it is obvious that one or more of us is trying to emphasize a certain aspect, and that will be my struggle this afternoon with you.

I want it clearly understood before I begin that what I am about to say to you is my own conviction and what I teach this afternoon is to be connected with me and with

me only. I do not represent a school here or a particular
congregation or a particular faction. I believe that factionism
is condemned in God's word. And so I begin today with a
struggle that I have noticed in all the speakers; that is, the
struggle with understanding how it is that one operates
within the framework of God's grace. Hundreds of brethren evidently have this same struggle or we would not be
discussing this subject.

It is the case that man must obey God and therein is
the dilemma. But I want to emphasize some good news to
us this afternoon. Yes, we must obey God, but I want to
emphasize that we *can* obey God. I want to turn our
attention, as brother Rubel just did a moment ago, to the
book of Romans and begin in the first chapter of Romans,
studying what I call the *harmony* of grace and law. I do not
believe we can read very far into the epistle to the Romans
and escape the emphasis that is placed upon the grace of
God and, more specifically, upon the justification by grace
through faith. Paul labels this message of justification
"good news" or "gospel" as it is translated, and he states
clearly in verse 1 that he has been separated unto the
proclamation of this new message. I understand that his
separation is from Judaism and even the religion of works,
humanly devised, that Paul knew in his Pharisee days. He
also understood that the Mosaic foundation on which he
had formerly stood had been abrogated (Gal. 2:19). You
will remember that Paul was a Pharisee (Acts 26:5). And it
is significant to me that this former Pharisee authored the
Roman letter showing a dramatic contrast between self-
complacency, set out in Luke 18 for instance, that some
sought through Phariseeism (Rom. 10:1-3), and the glory
of God's grace!

I believe there are some difficulties also discussed in the
Roman letter concerning the purpose or purposes of the
law of Moses as that law pertained to the gospel. The latter
discussion occupies much in the epistle.

But because Paul discusses the law of Moses, self-righteousness, and the gospel in the same epistle, some have concluded that all manner of law is now abrogated and that men are today wholly under grace in matters religious.[1] Such a teaching that one is wholly under grace and contributes nothing to his salvation is evidently anticipated by Paul in the very opening of the epistle when he writes (I am reading from the American Standard Version): "Through whom we receive grace and apostleship unto obedience of faith among all the nations for his name's sake" (Rom. 1:5). This obedience of faith, *hupakoee pisteos* 'the obedience of faith,' is the obedience to which faith leads and which perfects faith (Jas. 2:14-26). [Chart #1.] Paul is going to conclude this epistle to the Romans with the same idea (Rom. 16:26).

In an article called "The Obedience of Faith in the Letter to the Romans," Garlington notes that:

Chart #1

Romans 1:5

"εἰς ὑπακοὴν πίστεως" SUBJECTIVE GENITIVE; THE OBEDIENCE THAT BELONGS TO FAITH

Robertson: "THE OBEDIENCE WHICH SPRINGS FROM FAITH"

Vincent: "THE OBEDIENCE WHICH CHARACTERIZES AND SPRINGS FROM FAITH"

Denney: "OBEDIENCE TO THE FAITH: BUT ARGUES 'THE FAITH' IS NOT THE GOSPEL BUT THE STATE OF SALVATION"

Rienecker: "OBEDIENCE" (Quoting Otto Kuss, <u>Der Romer Brief</u>)

> The phrase [*hupakoee pisteos*] neatly summarizes Paul's apologetic in the letter . . . a programmatic statement of the main purpose of the Roman letter . . . a tool for obliterating distinction between Jew and Gentile.[2]

Garlington sees such obedience realized eschatologically, however.[3] But he nevertheless admits that the obedience under discussion springs from the faith that Paul preaches (Rom. 1:5). Since Garlington views salvation for the sinner living now as a faith-only proposition, he is driven to the *eschatos* to explain "obedience as the fundamental and decisive act of faith."[4] The phrase, *hupakoee pisteos*, is so strong, however, that even faith-only advocates cannot dismiss it. They must extrapolate the phrase to the second coming of Christ, because they know that every Jew and Gentile must one day have that obedience of faith. Even a faith-only advocate cannot get around this phrase. He must view the Jew and Gentile as being forced to obey in some millennial kingdom. Therefore, whatever one reads into the Roman text concerning law and grace must be tempered by an understanding from Romans 1:5 and 16:26 that obedience is an essential part of the system Paul emphasizes as superseding self-righteousness and the law of Moses.

The purpose for me this afternoon is to look at the textual background leading to Romans 5 and grace (which has already been well done, actually); then to make a reference to James 2 and the harmony so well set forth a moment ago. And finally I want to look at Romans 4 again to show us that all men from Adam to this one speaking right now are saved by grace through faith.

I believe the thesis of the Roman epistle is set forth in verses 16 and 17: "For I am not ashamed or confounded by the good news." One ought to look up that word *ashamed*. Paul says that this new message does not confuse him because "it is God's power to salvation to everyone that believes (keeps on believing) to the Jew first and also to the

Greek. For therein is a righteousness of God revealed from faith unto faith as it is written, But the righteous shall live by faith."

As already pointed out, *dikaiosune* is a key to Romans, the noun form given but the adjective being *dikaios* [Chart #2]. *Dikaios* is that which is right by God's order, apart from usage or custom as the profane Greek indicated.[5] In other words, Paul's *righteousness* is introduced into the

---

Chart #2

Romans 1:17a

For a Righteousness of God--

In it--

Is Being Revealed--

"δικαιοσυνη"

---

text in contrast to the common Greek usage as that *righteousness* which must be of God or about God. Righteousness, in the Greek mind, was a social virtue, but to Paul *righteousness* is a state inherent in the integrity of God and revealed in the gospel. Both the Gentile and the Jew had lived under systems that did not reveal the gospel righteousness belonging to God (Rom. 1:18-32; 2:1-29). Both Jew and Gentile are therefore concluded by the Old Testament Scriptures to be under sin before the time of the cross (Rom. 3:9,23). But now, apart from the law of Moses (Rom. 3:20,21), the system declaring God's righteousness has been made known. Let's note Romans 3:20 clearly. "Because by the works of the law shall no flesh be justified in his sight," cannot contain the idea that Paul was discussing any law whatsoever and that there is no law in the gospel system.[6] For, an earlier discussion of obedience (Rom. 1:5), an earlier discussion of judgment of men's deeds as those men obeyed the truth (Rom. 2:6,8), and a later discussion of the law of the spirit of life (Rom. 8:2) would be contradicted if Romans 3:20 is a reference to all law. The apostle Paul insisted that obedience was "according to my gospel" (Rom. 2:16), and one must conclude from the context of Romans 3:20 that Paul was contrasting the new gospel system with the law of Moses, not with just any law.

[Chart #3.] The theme of Romans is 1:17 and also the thesis. Paul takes the theme from Habakkuk 2:4. Habakkuk 2:4 originally was a reference to Israel's survival of the fate that awaited Babylon.[7] (In fact, the LXX adopted *ek pisteos mou*, while the Masoretic text has the Hebrew *be emunato* 'his faith'; LXX, "by my faith."[8] The former, that is the LXX, is first person, but the Masoretic is third masculine. All the old Latin manuscripts and the *G* and the *Ag* manuscripts read *emunati* which does not help us in trying to find out what Habakkuk originally meant because there is a waw-yod problem in transcription. But Isaiah 8:2 is helpful. If you will look in Isaiah 8:2, there the writer uses *emuna tam* 'their faith' confirming that the

---

Chart #3

"From Faith unto Faith"

Romans 1:17b

"εκ πιστεως"	Out of Faith
"εις πιστιν"	Into Faith

cf. Romans 3:30 as Paul concludes his discussion of his thesis of Romans 1:16,17.

"εκ πιστεως"	for the Jew
"δια της πιστεως"	for the Gentile

Why? Habakkuk 2:4 !

With the phrase, "from faith to faith" as idiomatic--
intensifying the idea of "by faith"

Masoretic text is right in Habakkuk 2:4, at least in my view, "but the just shall live by *his* faith." Paul's use of Habakkuk 2:4 as to the meaning of living by faith must therefore hold the meaning of the ancient writer's usage, *emunah*. Paul used that phrase in the way that Habakkuk used it. Listen carefully. *Emunah* means "unwavering hold to the word of God against all contrary opponents." That is what it means to live by faith and that is how the term *faith* is used in Genesis 15:6. Abraham held to the word of God against all contrary opponents and it was counted unto him for righteousness. Paul means in his thesis that the church's proclamation of the gospel cannot separate faith from faithfulness. Thus the good news of Christ for Jew and Gentile (Rom. 1:16,17; 3:29,30) is not that men are completely free from all law, but that the gospel system contains a law of faith that leads to God's justifying all men who obey (Rom. 3:27). Even the Jew and Gentile were justified by faith (Hab. 2:4), if they walked by that kind of faith while living under their former pre-cross system (Rom. 3:21,31). This last position is explained clearly in Romans 3:21-26, and I invite your attention to it at this time.

Romans 3:21-26 is one sentence in the original. This passage includes the vital thought that a righteousness of God was made known (perfect tense, "keeps on being made known") by a new system, but not by the law of Moses which law only witnessed, along with the prophets, to this new system. However, according to 3:21, this gospel message did and does make known God's righteousness (Rom. 3:21). Also this righteousness of God is *di pisteos* 'through faith, faith as the sphere of righteousness.' That is, man must be in the faith as in Christ (Gal. 3:13-27) to access the righteousness of God (2 Cor. 5:21). It is interesting to me to note that the LXX translation never translated any Hebrew word *remission*, for remission in the Old Testament was always in prospect (Rom. 3:21-23).

Notice that Paul says justification is freely (*dorean* 'as a gift') by grace as a *lutron* 'redemption or ransom' but only in Christ (Rom. 3:24). Therefore, as has been clearly pointed out today, man cannot earn his salvation, but man must be in Christ in order to have salvation, which Paul will explain in Romans 6. God's offer of his Son as the propitiation, the mercy seat (a word different from the one in 1 John 2:2) shows that God's forgiveness of any Gentile

---

Chart #4

FROM 95 THESES

Luther:

"It is not in the power of man's will to choose or reject whatever is offered to it."

(cf. Matt. 13:13-15)

"It is false to say that, if a man does all that he can, he removes the obstacles to grace."

(cf. Matt. 7:21)

"We do not become righteous by doing what is righteous; but having become righteous, we do what is righteous."

(cf. 1 John 2:29; 3:7)

"There is no form of reasoning (of syllogism) that holds with the things of God."

(cf. Isa. 1:18; 1 Thess. 5:21)

"It does not hence follow that the will is naturally depraves but . . . inclined toward evil . . . it is capable by the power [external grace, K. M.] of God of recovering."

(cf. Rom. 1:16,17)

"Man is a greater enemy to the grace of God than he is to the law itself."

(cf. Titus 2:11)

or Jew (Rom 3:25), who walked in obedient faith prior to the time of the cross, was forgiven in prospect. The gospel system proves that God was righteous in forgiving in prospect all the faithful of prior ages and that God is now the justifier of all the obedient today (Rom. 3:26). Brethren, sadly the majority of the Gentiles and Jews who lived prior to the cross were unforgiven. Only those who obeyed then (Hab. 2:4), who had that living faith, were eligible to receive the benefits of the crucifixion of Christ (Rom. 9-11; Eph. 2:10-12). That same obedient faith is necessary today (Rom. 8:1-3).

Let's take a moment now to talk about this so-called problem with Romans 5 and James 2. According to the preface (circa A.D. 1552) to his commentary on Romans, Martin Luther believed that *law* was that which no one could keep and that the only way one could keep God's commands was "from the bottom of his heart given by the Spirit." Luther added that "unbelief alone commits sin, and brings up the flesh . . . and God's grace just overlooks our sin until it can be slain at death." "Hence," Luther added, " . . . it comes that faith alone makes righteous, fulfills the law, for out of Christ's merit it brings the Holy Spirit."[9]

[Chart #4.] Notice these eight theses from Luther:

1. "It is not in the power of man's will to choose or reject whatever is offered to it." Matthew 13:13-15 rejects that notion.

2. "It is false to say that, if a man does all that he can, he removes the obstacles to grace." Jesus himself refutes that (Luke 19:10).

3. "We do not become righteous by doing what is righteous; but having become righteous, we do what is righteous." First John 2:29 contradicts that statement.

4. "There is no form of reasoning (of syllogism) that holds with the things of God." First Thessalonians 5:21 contradicts that.

5. "It does not hence follow that the will is naturally depraved but . . . inclined toward evil . . . and it is capable by the power [he means external grace] of God of recovering." The gospel system contradicts that.

6. And then in his thinking, Luther said: "Man is a greater enemy to the grace of God than he is to the law itself."[10] I used Titus 2:11 on the chart to show you that he was incorrect according to the Scriptures.

Now Luther, who thought that grace covered man's sins until man died without any effort on man's part, sounds different in his views from the words that Paul used in Romans 5:1,2.

> Being therefore justified by [*ek* 'out of'] faith, we have peace with God through our Lord Jesus Christ; through whom also we have had our access [as was pointed out a moment ago] by faith ["by faith" there has some uncertainty in the manuscripts, but nevertheless it is in most of our English translations] into this grace wherein we stand and we rejoice in hope of the glory of God.

One should note that grace must be accessed (*prosagoge* 'approached') out of faith. And I suggest this afternoon as has been well said today, the great blessing of the good news of Christ is that in him one can approach the grace of God.

Of course, Luther was reacting against the scholasticism and popular superstitions and abuses against the gospel of his day, and one might fancy Luther's arguments against rationalism today as ones which see obedience as legalism or ritualism. However, the vital issue today seems to be whether a man is hopeless to obey God, as Luther and Calvin taught, or whether a man has the ability to obey God and access the grace of God, which grace saves. Paul insists on the latter position in Romans 5:1,2.

Jack Lewis has noted that Luther's "faith alone" attitude toward grace caused Luther to insert *allein* (only) in Romans 3:28.[11] Those holding to faith alone cannot seem to distinguish between the system of faith apart from the works of the law of Moses which system of faith accesses grace (Rom. 5:1,2) and one's personal faith which is necessary to salvation but not the source "out of" which grace could be accessed. Paul's use of *faith* in Romans 5:1,2 is related to the gospel system Paul is discussing in contrast to works of the law of Moses (Rom. 3:28). Personal faith is a work of God (Jno. 6:28,29) and part of the gospel (Rom 10:9,10); but certainly personal faith would not be the source out of which access to the beautiful, awe-inspiring, humbling grace of God can be had. Only the gospel or "law of faith" as contrasted to the law of Moses can put one in Christ wherein is grace.

It is necessary for me to stop here for a moment and recognize the fact that some insist that in Romans Paul uses the term "law of Moses" as a synecdoche for the principle of any law.[12] This latter teaching heralds the idea that the annulling of the law of Moses is the annulling of the principle of law, or law, as a way to access justification. Such teaching must eventually run afoul of the term "law of faith" discussed above (Rom. 3:27). Also, the obedience of faith motivated by love does not conflict with God's grace according to Galatians 5:6. In fact, Christ tied together both law and love in the Old and New Testaments when he was asked the question: "What is the greatest commandment in the law? How readest thou? Thou shalt love the Lord thy God with all thy heart, soul, mind, and strength. And the second is like unto it; thou shalt love thy neighbor as thyself." If you do not remember anything else I have said today, try to remember this one line: Any faith, any love separated from obedience changes obedience to legalism. Paul is denying legalism in Romans, but he is not expunging law of any kind (Rom. 6:1,2). Yet some have said that while there is virtue in law, there is also failure in the law-based system. "The failure of law is not law. The failure of law is, I can't keep it."[13]

But Paul insists, brethren, on an access point into grace—obedient faith. It was shown above that the term *faith* in Romans 5:1,2 is a synecdoche for the gospel system (Rom. 1:16-3:18). If one could not keep, *could* not keep, God's commandments, one could not access grace, one could not love God (1 Jno. 5:3), and one could not live by faith because he would not have obedience (Rom. 1:5). Well, one can keep God's commandments from the heart, even under the law of Moses. Look at Luke 1:6. Zechariah and Elizabeth walked in *all* the commandments of the Lord, blameless. They lived under the law of Moses. And especially under the law of Christ, one can keep the commands of God or one cannot be said to live by faith (Rev. 3:17). One's keeping the commandments of God accesses justification but such obedience is not the source of one's salvation. It is not necessary to denigrate obedience nor grace to teach that the source of salvation is the latter and the access point is the gospel of faith. Law does not fail because "I can't keep it." I fail (Rom. 7).

Finally, the harmony of the passage known as James 2 seems to me to be in the fact that the Pauline usage of *faith* in Romans 5 and James' use of it is that James has under consideration the faith perfected by works. Note John C. Lodge's work.[14] In his discussion on faith and works as two different things, Lodge makes an interesting observation. He says (and he is talking about Dibelius' understanding of James):

> Dibelius' translation does have two corresponding active clauses: faith assisted, works perfected. The Greek does not. In the second clause of James 2:22, the text has the passive with *eteleiothe* as the subject following an instrumental prepositional phrase, *ek ton ergon*. The Greek does not accentuate *works* by making it the explicit subject. The emphasis by James, rather, falls upon "was perfected." Instead of faith and works as two subjects acting upon one another, faith acts and receives its wholeness or completion through works. The "iterative" imper-

fect (and here he tells us it is the only time used in the New Testament) implies the coexistence of faith in works in Abraham over a period, not the cooperation of two things. Thus the kind of correspondence that Dibelius finds between faith and works does not stand upon the Greek text of James 2:22. There is a distinct or stylistic correspondence between the two clauses of James 2:22 which Dibelius translates and does not obscure. The iterative imperfect underlies the true relationship between faith and works, knitting the two terms together at the center of a larger unit. Note that when James uses this phrase, "faith without works," his illustrations are Abraham and Rahab. Neither Abraham nor Rahab lived under the law of Moses, so James is not contrasting the gospel system, law of faith, with the works of the law of Moses' time which makes his discussion of a different force. James is insisting on the very nature of personal faith under any system as a faith that works.

We only have two ways to look at this, brethren, and I think these propositions (see Chart #5) by brother Thomas B. Warren set forth the matters before us very clearly. Either the Bible teaches that salvation from sin results from the grace of God alone, totally and completely apart from any human activity—and I did hear that today. Incidentally, sometimes I hear brethren say, "Well our brotherhood is just now finding grace." I have found hundreds of articles and sermon outlines by brethren through the years on just the subject of grace. We are not just discovering grace—or, the Bible teaches that salvation depends upon both the grace of God and the faithful loving obedience of the individual human being. It is at point two where we seem to be struggling. Well, since the syllogism sets forth the fact that *one* can not be the case, it must be *two*.

Let's take a moment now to look at the thought that all men are, or have been, saved by grace through faith. The thesis of the book of Romans is that any declaration from God as to righteousness involves faith (Hab. 2:4; Rom.

Chart #5

"EITHER"

The Bible teaches that salvation from sin results from the grace of God alone, totally and completely apart from any human activity.

"OR"

The Bible teaches that salvation depends upon both (1) the grace of God and (2) the faithful loving obedience of the individual human being.

"BUT"

1. If [A] salvation from sin is totally and completely by the grace of God with not "one whit" of human activity being involved at any point in the whole matter of salvation from sin by the grace of God, *then* [B] all human beings who have ever lived or who will yet live on the earth will be saved (John 3:16; Titus 2:11; Heb. 2:9; et.al.)

2. But it is *false* that [B] all human beings who have ever lived or who will yet live on the earth will be saved (Matt. 7:13,14; 25:31-46; 2 Thess 1:5-11; et.al.)

3. Therefore, it is *false* that [A] salvation from sin is totally and completely by the grace of God with not "one whit" of human activity being involved at any point in the whole matter of salvation from sin.

1:17). As we have already tried to point out, biblical faith is obedient faith: " . . . unto obedience of faith among all nations." And in any age one had to, or must, look to God for all hope of being righteous, for this is God's eternal purpose (Eph. 1:4; 3:11).

There are only two propositions, as we have already seen. Only one can be sound. Teachers of God's word have no other choices. Paul argues for obedient faith. Further, all men, if justified at all, are justified by grace in and through the precious gift of the blood of Christ (Rom. 3:24; Heb. 9:15). Because one's salvation is always by faith in another, all men's glorying is excluded:

> Where then is the glorying? It is excluded. By what manner of law? of works? No, but by a law of faith. We reckon therefore that a man is justified by faith apart from the works of the law (Rom. 3:27).

Romans 4 was written to prove these points as set forth in Romans 3:27,28 and to show what "by faith" means. [Chart #6.]

If anyone had reason to glory in his accomplishments, Abraham did. "What shall we say then that Abraham, our

---

Chart #6

'ALL' (OT & NT)   ROMANS 4

SAVED BY GRACE

THROUGH FAITH

ROM. 1:16-17 ANY DECLARATION FROM GOD AS TO RIGHTEOUSNESS INVOLVES FAITH.

IN ANY AGE ONE MUST (HAD TO) LOOK TO GOD FOR HIS HOPE -- EPH. 3:11; 1:4 ETERNAL PURPOSE

ALL ARE JUSTIFIED BY GOD'S GRACE -- ROM. 3:24, THROUGH THE BLOOD OF CHRIST -- HEB. 9:15; ROM. 3:26,28

ALL MEN'S GLORYING IS EXCLUDED -- ROM. 3:27. SINCE HIS SALVATION IS ALWAYS "BY FAITH" IN ANOTHER -- ROM. 3:28

ROM. 4 WAS WRITTEN TO PROVE THE ABOVE POINT, AND TO SHOW WHAT "BY FAITH" MEANS.

forefather, hath found according to the flesh?" That phrase, "according to the flesh," gives commentators fits because of a placement problem in manuscripts. But note here, at least, that Abraham was chosen from a world population and promised a multiple inheritance (Gen. 12:1-3). He is called the "friend" of God, "father of the faithful" who did the works of God (Jas. 2:23; Jno. 8:39). His name became a euphemism for paradise, and he is memorialized by several Bible writers, including Luke (Lk. 16:23). If anyone could be seen as having earned his salvation as a reward, surely it should have been Abraham. (See Chart #7.)

But Abraham was not justified on the grounds of his works (Rom. 4:28). If Abraham's works had been the source of justification, Abraham would have been reported as having earned his reward. But the Scripture still states that "Abraham believed God and it was counted unto him [or reckoned unto him, or credited unto him] for righteousness" (Rom. 4:3). That is, the statement originally recorded in Genesis 15:6 precludes our deducing that Abraham merited justification. Abraham's righteousness, which is a legal term as Paul uses it, had to be given to him on account (Rom. 4:4,5). This legal justification of a believer is compared to being forgiven (Rom. 4:6-8). Therefore, Abraham's justification by God was based on God's grace and received by Abraham's faith (Rom. 4:5). This faith, as discussed in Romans, included obedience and induces obedience. To illustrate further the unmerited nature of declared righteousness, Paul states that such a blessing did not require circumcision. To those who hold that in Romans Paul is contrasting *any* law with the gospel, let it be respectfully noted that Paul used Abraham as illustrative of the kind of faith that can be declared righteous (Rom. 4:13-15). [Chart #8.] But Abraham would not have needed to be declared righteous if he had no sin (Rom. 4:15b), and that tells me there was a law in existence at that time. Justification by God does not

---

Chart #7

IF ANY MAN HAD REASON TO GLORY IN HIS OWN ACCOMPLISHMENTS, ABRAHAM DID – 4:1 (cf. JOHN 8:39).

BUT, ABRAHAM WAS <u>NOT</u> JUSTIFIED ON THE GROUNDS OF <u>HIS</u> "WORKS" – 4:2-8

   1. <u>EARNED</u> REWARD THEN, IF BY <u>HIS</u> WORKS – v3

   2. GEN. 15:6 PRECLUDES SUCH MERIT – v4

   3. HIS <u>LEGAL</u> RIGHTEOUSNESS (JUSTIFICATION) WAS "*LOGIZOMAI*" TO HIM.

ABRAHAM'S JUSTIFICATION WAS BASED ON:

   1. GOD'S GRACE RECEIVED BY FAITH – v5

   2. FAITH <u>INCLUDES</u> OBEDIENCE – <u>AND</u> FAITH <u>INDUCES</u> OBEDIENCE (ROM. 16:25,26; HEB. 11:8-19; JAS. 2:21-24)

   3. THE "IMPUTATION" OF SUCH RIGHTEOUSNESS (JUSTIFICATION) DEPENDS ON GOD'S WILLINGNESS TO FORGIVE SINS – vv 6-8

   4. THIS "IMPUTATION" IS THE RIGHTEOUSNESS OF GOD (i.e. JUSTIFICATION DECLARED) – ROM. 1:17; 3:21 – NOT THE PERSONAL RIGHTEOUSNESS OF CHRIST – ROM. 5:9,10; 4:11

   5. <u>NOT BASED</u> ON CIRCUMCISION (GEN. 15:6 = 17:24 BY 29 YEARS) – TYPE OF SAVED TODAY WHETHER CIRCUMCISED OR NOT -- vv 9-12

---

exclude obedience to law, but justification must include obedient faith under any system (Rom. 4:16).

The prototype of the faith that accesses grace is Abraham's (Rom. 4:17ff). Abraham's faith looked beyond human circumstances. Abraham acted on what God spoke. In the second place, according to Romans 4:18, Abraham acted because of what God spoke. (The context of Romans 4:17 deals with the conception of Isaac.) And in the third

---

Chart #8

THE INSTRUMENT OF JUSTIFICATION WAS NOT THE LAW OF MOSES. (4:13-15.) JUSTIFICATION DOES <u>NOT</u> <u>EXCLUDE</u> OBEDIENCE TO LAW, BUT MUST <u>INCLUDE</u> FAITH (4:16).

ABRAHAM'S FAITH = OUR PROTOTYPE

    1. LOOKS BEYOND HUMAN CIRCUMSTANCES — 4:17,18

    2. BECAUSE OF "THAT WHICH WAS SPOKEN" — 4:18 (GEN. 12:1-4; 15:5)

    3. NOT WEAK — 4:19

    4. FILLED WITH HOPE, FULL ASSURANCE — 4:20,21

    5. BASIS FOR GOD'S DECLARING HIM RIGHTEOUS — 4:22

SPECIAL SIGNIFICANCE FOR ALL CHRISTIANS
4:23-25

FOR: JESUS WAS "RAISED AGAIN FOR OUR JUSTIFI-CATION"

---

place, Abraham acted with full knowledge of his own deadness, yet with the full assurance of hope in God's promise (Rom. 4:20,21). Abraham knew in his deadness that if he did what God spoke, he (Abraham) would be given life. Abraham and Sarah had to come together *by faith* in order to receive the blessing of a son in their old age. It is without doubt, and I do not mean to be facetious by this, that Isaac was not conceived by grace only, promise only, or faith only. Abraham and Sarah accessed God's promise. Note clearly that Abraham had to act out of his own deadness to appropriate God's grace. That is why, when I started this today, I said, "The news is, we must obey God. The good news is, we can; Abraham did." Out of his own deadness, he acted on, because of, and with full assurance of the hope of God.[16] [Chart #9.]

Righteousness denotes the condition in which one is right with God. This condition is declared by God, not by man (Rom. 3:21-26), and is legally imputed to man by or through obedient faith (Rom. 1:5). The primary import of *dikaiosunee* is a change of position and not a change of condition. One who is pardoned of criminal guilt is not a valuable citizen until that one does right, and to be righteous, one must also do right as Abraham did.

Chart #9

ALL IN AGES: SAVED BY GRACE THROUGH FAITH — NOT BY LAW THROUGH WORKS

ROM. 4:16; EPH 2:8

BUT, THE ONLY FAITH THAT EVER IS DECLARED JUSTIFIED IS THAT FAITH WHICH RESPONDS TO WHAT GOD SAYS

ROM. 10:17; 4:3	FAITH	WORK OF FAITH 2 THESS. 1:11
	AND	
JAS. 2:21-24	ACTION	GAL. 5:6

A LIVING FAITH <u>PRODUCES</u> WORKS — JAS. 2:24

BUT, SALVATION IS NOT *EX ERGON* (EPH. 2:9; TITUS 3:5) "OUT OF WORKS" OR *EX NOMOU* (PHIL. 3:9a) "OUT OF LAW." SALVATION IS *EK THEOU* (PHIL. 3:9b) "OUT OF GOD."

IT IS HOW A PERSON CONCEIVES OF THE SOURCE OF HIS SALVATION THAT MAKES ALL THE DIFFERENCE!!!

WORKS AS A <u>GROUNDS</u> OF SALVATION — EXCLUDED (ROM. 4:2-5).

WORKS AS <u>CONDITIONS</u> OF SALVATION — INCLUDED (ACTS 20:34,35). THIS IS HOW CHRISTIANITY IS LAW.

Chart #10

<u>WHY DISCUSS THE OBVIOUS?</u>
THERE IS AN OBEDIENCE THAT IS INHERENT IN FAITH
AND THERE ARE WORKS THAT EXPRESS FAITH (ROM.
1:5; 16:26; cf. ACTS 10:34,35; JAS. 2:20-24).

WHY DO SOME QUESTION OBEDIENCE; ESPECIALLY
SINCE ALL CHRISTIANS ARE THOSE WHO LOVINGLY
OBEY CHRIST (JNO. 14:15)?

Romans and James are not contradictory but in harmony. The former treats of a system or law of faith in contrast to the law Moses. The latter book treats of the kind of faith, a "completing" faith that is alive and blessed by God.

The Jews had perverted the law of Moses, brethren, by thinking of their keeping the law as meriting justification. The Jews' prophets and Paul insist that the just, however, must live by obedient faith—Abrahamic faith.

I have a question for us this afternoon. I am wondering why we are discussing the obvious. [Chart #10.] Do not all of us realize that to love God means that we keep his commandments? What is being said among us that makes this kind of a discussion necessarily taking place? When I was growing up in the Presbyterian Church, as a little boy I was told that if God elected me, chose me, did it for me, I would be saved. But that little boy, until he was twenty-six years old, lived in fear of almighty God. Abject fear! Sometimes I could not sleep at night because I never really knew—was I one of God's elect? Somebody knocked on my door in 1965 from Abilene Christian University and said, "May we talk to you about Jesus?" "What do you want to tell me? You can obey God and God will save you. Tell me that. That's what I want to hear."

Now brethren, I know that sometimes we overemphasize some things, but I have never heard a gospel preacher from that time until now tell me that I could earn my salvation. Gospel preachers always told me that if I would submit myself to God, God would save me. That is coming out of darkness into light. I want to beg us as a brotherhood never to dilute that message because there are people out there who are afraid of almighty God, and we have some good news. My friend, you can obey God. You can do it. You will not save yourself, but you can do what God intends you to do.

Paul started with the obedience of faith. I want to suggest something to you very quickly. I am saying this to the whole brotherhood. For the last couple of years I have been studying what is called faith development theory developed by Dr. James Fowler of Emory University. I have been wondering why our brethren seem to be so upset about grace and law and are so determined to rebel against restorationism. Their "faith development" appears to be stymied. Note what was said about a Dr. Crisp.

I want you to concentrate on this statement from Benjamin Brook's *Lives*:

> Persons who have embraced sentiments which afterwards appear to them to be erroneous, often think they can never remove too far from them; and the more remote they go from their former opinions, the nearer they come to the truth, they think. This was unhappily the case with Dr. Crisp. His ideas of the grace of Christ had been exceedingly low, and he had imbibed sentiments which produced in him a legal and self-righteous spirit. Shocked at the recollection of his former views and conduct, he seems to have imagined that he could never go far enough from them.

Some today seem to be as Dr. Crisp! Brethren, brethren, brethren, let's not be stymied in the faith that we *can* keep God's commands (1 Jno. 2:3).

Endnotes

1. James Massey, "How Galatians Means Me," n.p., n.d., sound cassette. Refer also to Rubel Shelly, "The Antinomy of Law and Grace," n.p., 1990, Nashville, TN: Sound Cassette.

2. D. B. Garlington, "The Obedience of Faith in the Letter to the Romans, Part I: The Meaning of υπακωη πιστεως," *Wesleyan Theological Journal* 52 (Fall 1990): 201-02.

3. Ibid., 205.

4. Ibid.

5. For a thorough discussion of these forms see Gottlob Schrenk, "*dikh*," in *Theological Dictionary of the New Testament*, ed. Gerhard Kittle, trans. and ed. Geoffrey Bromiley (Grand Rapids: Wm. B. Eerdmans, 1964), 2:174-225.

6. This point is well discussed by George Vandervelde in "The Grammar of Grace: Karl Rahner as a Watershed in Contemporary Theology," *Theological Studies* 49 (September 1988): 445-59.

7. TB. Makkot 23b.

8. David S. Dockery, "The Use of Hab. 2:4 in Rom. 1:17: Some Hermeneutical and Theological Considerations," *Wesleyan Theological Journal* 22 (Fall 1987): 24-36.

9. See J. H. Merle O'Aubigne, "The Life and Times of Martin Luther," trans. H. White in *Tyndale Series of Great Biographies* (Chicago: Moody Press, n.d.) for a discussion of Luther's approach.

10. Ibid.

11. Jack Lewis, "Faith Alone," *Gospel Advocate* 128 (6 March 1986): 145-48.

12. Massey, "How Galatians Means Me," Sound Cassette.

13. Shelly, "The Antinomy of Law and Grace," Sound Cassette.

14. John C. Lodge, "James and Paul at Cross-Purposes? James 2:22," *Biblica* 62 (1981): 195-213.

15. Ibid., 199-200.

16. Lewis, "Faith Alone," pp.145-148.

Question-Answer Session

Panelists

Moderator: I am amazed that this many people have even changed locations and we are beginning the last session on time. I need to explain one or two things before we go into the question period so you will know what to expect, at least in terms of the order. I will call upon the group leaders to state the questions that have come out of those groups. This is not an open forum. You have had, in a sense, a forum where you have talked in your groups and the only questions we are going to entertain during this period are the questions that were generated by the groups. That is what we stated at the beginning of the day and we will maintain that format. Quite frankly, in the hour and a quarter we have, the panel probably could not deal with all the questions that came out of the discussion group here in the auditorium. So I will ask the group leaders, one at a time, to ask one question. That will be addressed either to one person who has been a speaker or to two of them or, in perhaps one or two cases, all of them.

When we shall have gone through all of the groups, then we will start over again until we run out of time. I hope you will not be disappointed if we do not get to your question. It may be that person number two who asks a question will ask the question that person number five is planning to ask, in which case he goes to another question that was generated from his group. And it is hoped that by having the resource persons respond to the questions which have been generated in the discussion groups, we will try to get at the nerve of the issue, the extent to which men have agreed or disagreed, so we can have further clarification. I will stay up here and monitor the situation. We may begin now with the first questioner.

Question: *To John Mark Hicks. Please give us a better definition of what you mean by* progressive sanctification.

Hicks: Progressive sanctification is simply a distinction that refers to the process of growth or the amount of growth. When we become Christians we are infants. We are immature. We grow. We grow in the fruit of the Spirit. We grow in personal holiness. We grow in learning truths so that we approximate more and more what the image of Christ is. As we start out, we may be very low in terms of approximating the image of Christ. But as we grow in the grace and in the knowledge of the Lord, as we learn more, as we are able to implement more in our lives, through the empowerment of God, we become more and more like Jesus Christ. And that is basically what I mean by progressive sanctification.

Now maybe implicit in the question is that there is a sense in which sanctification is a one-time, definitive sort of thing, and in that way is synonymous with justification. We are all saints in the sight of God. Paul's letters address us as saints in Christ. And so we stand holy in the presence of God. But in our personal lives, we are not perfect and we seek to grow. We attempt to approximate more and more what the image of Christ is by becoming more like him in our lives. So on one hand we are saints; we are made holy in God's sight; we are declared holy in God's sight; we are separated from the world and from sin. But in another sense, in our daily lives, we are constantly in a process of struggle against sin, struggle against Satan, and we are attempting to grow and become more and more like Jesus Christ every day. I hope that is sufficient.

Question: *This question is to Rubel Shelly. In Paul's use of the law, is he arguing against the law of Moses or any law? How does that fit in in light of a statement that you made, or it was heard in your statement, that there is no law at all? What about the law of Christ or the law of faith?*

Shelly: To begin, I do not recall making a statement that there is no law. My statement would be the same as Paul's that the commandments, *every* commandment, is holy and righteousness and good. James refers to the "perfect law of liberty" that we, within a grace system, look to and depend upon. My point is not, never has been, that we are not accountable to law. That is not Paul's point.

The point is that, accountable to law as we are, our justification is not based on our ability to perform adequately under law. That is Paul's point. Paul says the law is holy. Every commandment is good. The problem is, I am unholy. I am "sold under sin"; I am a "slave to sin." So in Romans generally, when Paul is talking about the relationship of law to justification, in my opinion he probably has in mind principally the law that he had struggled with, which is the law of Moses. And yet the point that is made in his argument in the book of Romans is that law against whatever background one comes from—because, remembering chapters 1 and 2, he spoke not only to the Jews but to the moralists and even to the pagan who had the law written on his heart—and he says the law is not the ground of our justification. The law exposes sin for what it is, shows sin to be the agent of our destruction. The law marks, we would say, the land mines that we are most likely to step on to destroy ourselves. And we are always accountable to law. Paul never said, nor have I, that we are not accountable to law. It is because we *are* accountable to law that we are manifest before God as sinners. But his argument within the book of Romans is that, since law is holy and we are unholy, the basis for our justification must be something other than the ability to keep law. So for the sake of his argument, it does not really matter which law it is.

Grant for the moment, as I think it is, that it is principally the law of Moses. Let it be whichever one you want it to be, let it be extended by principle—as I did in my speech—to cover any law as a system leading to righteousness, even using the gospel as a legalism. That can be done.

You see, as Keith pointed out in his speech, even under the Old Testament, justification was not by law keeping. The righteous were living "by faith" even then. These people who, under law, were obligated to the commandments were failing in their obedience—just as Abraham, believing God, was credited for righteousness. One chapter later, he sins in connection with the birth of Ishmael, but God does not disallow his promise, God does not set aside his promise. Abraham was subject to law; he broke law. His justification, however, came not by his ability to keep law but, in spite of his manifest inability to do so. He was saved by virtue of God's faithfulness. He was saved by grace.

The original question as asked is: Which law do I think it is? In the book of Romans, most often I believe the reference is to the law of Moses. By extension, the principle relates to any law, including using the New Testament as a legalism. And Paul says rule keeping, law keeping is not the ground for justification. The ground of justification is God's grace as we access it by faith. Faith means that we acknowledge that there is a law there. Faith means that we accept its obligations upon ourselves. Faith means that we try to keep the law. Grace means, in spite of our inability to do so perfectly, the faithful and gracious God saves us by mercy and lovingkindness, just as he did Abraham, just as he did David, just as he does us.

Moderator: For the sake of recording I will ask, are there any other panel members who would like to comment on this? Keith Mosher does.

Mosher: I sense, although I am not sure because I have not talked to him personally, that there is a basic disagreement here between me and Rubel on this point. And it has to do with this law that is in the New Testament. I do not believe that Paul is teaching that we cannot keep any law or that men never did keep law. I hear, sometimes, brethren say that Jesus was the only one who kept the law of Moses perfectly. I do not know what is meant by that, but it implies that if a man had been perfect in his nature and had kept the law of Moses, he, by the law of Moses, could have been saved. And brethren, I want us to understand that nobody, if he had kept it perfectly, could have been saved by the law of Moses. It is impossible that the blood of bulls and goats should take away sin (Heb.

10:1-4). Men *kept* the law of Moses. That is the point I was trying to get across today. You look at Luke 1:6 in your Bibles; read it. Elizabeth and Zacharias walked in all the commandments of the Lord blameless. You look at Philippians 3:8 in your Bible. Paul in his respects to the law was blameless, but his law keeping under that system left him in an imperfect state. But the law of faith says that when I obey the gospel, I am perfected in Christ (2 Cor. 5:21). That is how Christianity is law. In Romans 4:16 we are told that all, in all ages, are saved by grace through faith, not by law through works; but the only faith that ever is declared justified is that faith which responds to what God says. Salvation is not *ek ergon*. Salvation is *ek theou* 'out of God' (Phil. 3:9). And how I conceive of that source of salvation makes the difference. It needs also to be mitigated by the idea that my obedience it absolutely essential to being placed in the position where God will justify me. In that sense, Christianity is law.

Woodson: C. D. F. Moule in *Essays in New Testament Interpretation* has a very splendid chapter on exactly this point. I refer to this statement. He says, concerning Paul: " . . . the vital distinction is not between law in itself, whether as a code or as a ground of obligation but between two different attitudes to, and uses of, law—on the one hand, the recognition of law as a revelation of God's will and purpose, and, on the other hand, to attempt to use it 'legalistically' to establish one's own righteousness" (C. F. D. Moule, *Essays in New Testament Interpretation*, 1982: 265). And where those two concepts are not kept distinct, there is inevitable confusion. There is a difference between a legalistic keeping of the law of Moses, the law of Christ, or any other law, and respecting the gospel of Jesus Christ as God's word and submitting to it from the heart. That is not legalism. That is not works-righteousness. That is not keeping the law of Moses. And to imply or state that there is no distinction and that all law is always legalism is, in my judgment, a statement that is not found in the book of Romans or anywhere else. I still await the discussion of the law of faith and the law of the spirit of life who has made me free from the law of sin and death. That is not legalism. That is not the law of Moses. That is the gospel of our Lord Jesus Christ, a very, very important distinction.

Question: *Perhaps moving a little bit off of the subject of grace, works, and law, but nonetheless connected with one of the speeches that was made earlier, the group that I was associated with this morning wanted a question addressed to Rick Oster with regard to his comments in light of Romans 5:5. The question would be phrased in this fashion: How do we receive the Spirit? Does the Spirit give us faith and, if so, in what way does the Spirit give us faith?*

Oster: Your question really has two parts, and I think one is more difficult to answer than the other. It is like saying, does God answer prayer and, if so, how? As I tried to point out this morning, if one just looks in the Greek concordance under *pistis*, the Greek noun that is sometimes translated *faith* or *faithfulness*, it is very clear that in Galatians 5 it is a fruit of the Spirit. And Romans 12 talks about faith being given. In Ephesians 6 I tried to make the point but I really did not have time to expand on it. I am talking about these being godly attributes and characteristics and things that the Christian needs that are given to the Christian as a child of God. The way we receive the Spirit is when we obey the gospel; Acts 2:38 is a good example of that, as are other texts. It is just an example of the way the Spirit of God, life of the child of God, bears fruit and helps mature the

Christian. This would relate to some of the discussion earlier about sanctification—the Christian being brought more into conformity with the image of Christ.

In terms of the mechanics of it, I cannot tell you how any of those mechanics work that have anything to do with the inner man. As Paul makes very clear, that is an unseen world which is, of the two worlds, far more important to the Christian than the seen world. Our hope and confidence eternally is based on the truths and principles of the unseen world, and I really cannot tell you the mechanics of how things work in the unseen world in terms of the inner man or the Spirit of God and things like that. I know that it does because the Bible teaches it that way, but beyond that I really cannot go much further any more than I can tell you how, in Romans 8, the Spirit of God always intercedes and really helps me pray my prayers. The Bible says he does it and I believe that. I cannot draw a diagram—perhaps some can. I am not as skilled in diagrams to show you what that would look like or to explain it better.

Question: *John Mark Hicks, there were some folks, in fact thirty-nine of us in one group, who wanted to hear some elaboration on this idea of submissive faith. You made a distinction between submissive faith and doing our best. But the question was brought out, how far off the mark, to put it in a negative way, may one be; or to put it more positively, how perfect or mature must one be before he can be confident that he indeed has this submissive faith. Maybe intention is another word. In fact, that word came up a good bit. Give us a little background on submissive faith that will help clarify that for some folks.*

Hicks: The intent of using the phrase *submissive faith* is simply to say that our disposition before God of trust and affection for Jesus Christ is such that when we come to a command of God, it is our intention to submit to that command. Our faith is willing to yield to his will over our will. The classic example is the passage we discussed in James 2. Abraham was justified by faith when he offered Isaac. When faith submits, faith saves. Faith submits when faith yields to God's will rather than yielding to our own will. And so my point about my submissive faith is the same point that Keith was making about obedient faith. I could have used that phrase. Obedient faith is a synonymous term here, but I did want to introduce a term that is not as familiar in order to stress the point that the essence of faith is the willingness to submit our will to God's will and the intention of doing whatever God asks us to do. That is the kind of faith I am talking about. That faith is given evidence, it is made perfect (Jas. 2), when it actually does submit, not when it just thinks about submitting but when it actually does submit. I believe that by your own consciousness of your faith, you can know within yourself whether you have the kind of faith that is willing to submit. Now we all recognize that even though we are sometimes willing, we do not do it. Paul said it in Romans 7.

Sometimes we are willing to obey, but we do not always do it. We do not always do what we know to do. This is the point about doing your very best. The fact that we do sometimes sin indicates that we do not always do our best. When you sin you are not doing your best. You are not doing what God is enabling you to do; you are not doing your best when you sin. Whether it be sins of omission or commission, as ministers of the word, we all know that we have struggles of doubt over whether we should be sitting here watching *Star Trek* or whether we should be out visiting and evangelizing the lost. We struggle with that. And sometimes maybe we do not have a certain feeling as to whether we are doing the exact thing we need to be doing at that particular time. But I am confident about my faith such that I intend to do what I know to do. I submit myself through faith. I act upon my faith in submission to God, and that is the focal point of what I wanted to stress.

Woodson: I think this matter of intention to the exclusion or the omission of obedience is a very, very significant thing to think about. I am reading a quotation from a brother in Christ. So far as I know, he is not present so I shall not call his name. Here is what he says concerning what he terms "a spirit of obedience":

> With firm conviction and heavy hearts . . . we renounce as false and unhealthy doctrine, contrary to and unworthy of the gospel of Jesus Christ, the teaching that says that there are those who cast themselves on the grace of God as manifested in Jesus Christ, and in the spirit of obedience do all they know to do and believe all they know to believe to be pleasing to the Lord, and yet are still not worthy of the name Christian or of the fellowship of the church of Christ . . . (Ron Highfield, "Hermeneutical Fragments," Christian Scholars' Conference, July 1990: 11).

Now think about that for a moment. "The spirit of obedience." Now what is "the spirit of obedience"? Is it just an intention? Is it just a kind of general idea that I want to be a good citizen, I want to be a good person? Or does the spirit of obedience actually do what God has taught that person to do to become a Christian and to live the Christian life, not in the sense of legalism as we have already discussed, but as a guiding of our service to God? Tomorrow, if you have not done it yet, you had better send your income tax in. It will not do to say, "I had the spirit of obedience and that is all that was expected of me." Your next address will be in Atlanta.

Question: *Several people in our group thought that our speakers were closer together than originally thought. But several also had some difficulty, Rubel, with some of the things they understood you to be saying having to do with this! When you say there is nothing we can do to effect our salvation—that may not be exactly the way you would say it—are you including faith? If so, is faith nothing? And what does Luke 13:3 mean concerning repentance? This is something we must do, repent or perish (Rev. 20:12). We are judged according to our works. In Acts 10:48, they were commanded to be baptized; 2 Thessalonians 1:8, those who obey not the gospel are lost; 2 Peter 1:6-11, Christians were told to make every effort to add the Christian graces and that was in order to make your calling and election sure. And James 2:24 was brought up—being justified by works. How do you put all that together?*

Shelly: As I indicated in the paper earlier, righteousness is discussed in Scripture from two standpoints. There is the *dikaiosune* of right standing before God. Then there is the *dikaiosune* of ethical behavior that is the lived-out experience of discipleship. I am aware of all the passages that were just cited and can lengthen the list; I used several of those very passages in my paper. When I say there is nothing that we contribute to our salvation, when I say that our salvation arises from the grace of God alone, I am discussing and identifying *dikaiosune* as right standing before God and the ground of that status.

As I understand Scripture, we contribute not one whit to the purchase price of our redemption. That is a free gift. That is given to us. That is why it is called grace. That is why it is not given to us as debt or wages paid for anything that we have done. And persons who have thought they have heard me say that grace means, salvation by grace entails, that we do not even have to believe the gospel, we do not have to repent of our sins, we do not have to be baptized, we do not have to grow in faith, we do not pray, we do not share the gospel, that is altogether foreign to what I have said or Paul has affirmed with regard to righteousness as the lived experience of faith. As the lived experience of our faith, we acknowledge those commandments. We have this attitude of submissiveness, both in intent and behavior.

But folks, in obeying those commandments we are not contributing to the ground of our salvation. The ground of our salvation is provided at the cross and by the work of Christ alone. Our salvation arises from, it is rooted in, it grows out of, it comes to full blossom in Christ. The gift that is being given to us freely is put in the box, wrapped and the bow tied entirely by God's doing. It arises from the grace of God alone. We do not contribute one whit. We accept it (Rom. 5:2); we have access into it by faith. In our faith which is, back to the speech, living faith, surrendered faith, submissive faith, access faith, obedient faith, in our repentance and baptism; in our Christian discipleship, we are not contributing anything to our salvation. We are, in that act of faith and surrender, acknowledging in the only way (Jas. 2) that a person who says he believes can acknowledge, show it by something that happens in your life. Show it by a deed; show it by surrender. We are not contributing anything to the ground of our salvation. We are, in fact, evidencing our acceptance of the free gift, the free gift, that has been provided entirely on the basis of the finished work of Christ at the cross. So soteriologically salvation is, righteousness is the free gift of God, right standing, offered on the basis of the blood of Christ alone. We contribute nothing to that. We have our access into that by faith, this obedience to the gospel that we have all talked about, so that in accepting it we contribute nothing to it, but in accepting it we do so in the only way faith can ever show itself, that is, by something that evidences that faith. And the three markers, historically, are baptism, and the Lord's supper, and proclamation of gospel. So every use of Paul in Romans of *dikaiosune* as the free gift of right standing before God is predicated on what Christ alone has done. Our response to that in obedient faith is not making a contribution to it, is not finishing out what God has started—God puts us at eight on the ladder and we climb nine and ten. It is a free gift of God, and in our faith by which we have access into it, we accept it through our surrender, submission, obedience to the gospel.

Mosher: I want to recommend a book to you by Zane Hodges. It is a study of faith and works. *The Gospel Under Siege: A Study of Faith and Works*, 1981. Now Hodges argues in that book that if works are essential to salvation, one could never be sure of one's salvation until death. We have not asked the question today, but we need to ask it: "Are works essential to salvation?" Absolutely. Hodges is in error. What kind of works? Acts 10:34,35. Only when we obey God, as I tried to say in my speech earlier, are we saved. I think sometimes in trying to overemphasize what we perceive to be a flaw in our former way of doing things, we run so far from it that we throw the baby out with the bath water, as Rick said this morning. There are works that are essential to salvation, and my contention is that Paul teaches us in Romans that we can do those things. We *can do* those things. In our imperfection, we can do them. That is why Abraham is the illustration. I have never believed that I had a perfect baptism. For all I know, the guy left one hair out of the water, I do not know. But I was baptized. I repented. What do we mean by some of these terms concerning "perfection"? I did not hear a lot of definitional terms and I think I was guilty of that today. But there are works that are essential to salvation, and maybe that is the question we should have asked (Acts 10:34,35).

Woodson: If the statement concerning contributing one whit to our salvation refers to the divine side of salvation such as the death, burial, and the resurrection of Christ, the following questions must be answered: Who holds that by what he or she or they can do they will contribute one whit to the death, burial, and resurrection of Christ? Who does that? Also, in the same context where this statement occurred in the *Arbeit Macht Frei!* statement—this question needs to be asked and answered because in the very next sentence after the statement concerning not contributing "one whit": "*Arbeit Macht Frei!* is the falsehood against which both Romans and Galatians protest." Now where in Romans and Galatians does Paul protest against anyone who thought he could contribute one whit to the divine side of salvation? Where in Romans or Galatians does Paul protest against anyone who was trying to contribute one whit to the death, the burial, and resurrection of Christ? If one cannot demonstrate that those opposed in Romans and Galatians were seeking to supplement the divine side of salvation, at least to contribute one whit to it, the reference in Romans and Galatians cannot be made to allude to the divine side, but must refer to the human side. And brethren, you know as well as I do that this is where what is called the "outrageous and slanderous lie" is found. Where in Ephesians 2:1-10 or elsewhere does Paul protest against anyone attempting to contribute one whit to the divine side of salvation? Where is there a commentator other than the writer of *Arbeit Macht Frei!* who claims the books of Romans and Galatians were a protest against the efforts of anyone to contribute one whit to the divine side of salvation? I believe the idea that our people or anybody else is attempting to contribute one whit to the finished work of Christ on the cross is not accurate. And there, it seems to me, is a matter that needs to be considered. Thank you.

Moderator: I was in hopes Rubel would comment, at least one whit, on this; but I had said in our questions period that we were not here to discuss things that these men had written elsewhere. I do feel in this case it would probably contribute to an understanding of what Rubel has been saying today, right or wrong, if he would respond. And so I hope he will comment on that point.

Shelly: I think the general consensus of commentaries that I have ever read on Romans and Galatians and Ephesians 2 express precisely the sentiment that Paul is inveighing against is the notion that salvation is somehow something that God does a percentage of and we finish out, that, in fact, we contribute to the ground of our justification.

It seems to me difficult to understand Ephesians 2:8,9 any other way. "It is by grace you have been saved, through faith, and this not from yourselves." Why Paul! Nobody ever thought that. *Somebody must have!* Paul is responding to it. "It is by grace you have been saved through faith, and this not from yourselves; it is the gift of God, not by works so that no one can boast." Paul believed that there was somebody somewhere who thought that somehow salvation was "from yourselves" rather than the gift of God, and there were certain things which, if we did it, we would have the right to "boast" before God. If he does not know someone that he names in the passage, he at least hypothetically raises the possibility; that is one way the gospel could be understood. And I certainly do, in fact, understand that that is what Romans (in expanded version) and Galatians (as the "Reader's Digest Condensed Version") inveigh against.

In Galatians 1:6-9, when he says there are some people "anathema from God," they are precisely those people who, as Paul says are "leaving the gospel I preached to you." In what way? You are leaving the gospel I preached which was a faith system—an access by faith into grace wherein ye stand—and making it into a legalism that he explores in detail in chapter 5 and talks about specific things. They had said, "Now in addition to your repentance and baptism, you have to embrace circumcision and the dietary laws. You have this to 'contribute' to your justification. Otherwise, what you have done to this point through faith in your repentance and baptism has only got you half way home to being a Christian." You know, I can plead perfectly guilty for having misunderstood Ephesians 2 and Galatians and Romans. Folks, I am not the only person who has ever read Romans that way. The standard commentaries that I have read all through my life are the ones that deal with that very problem; and I believe, in fact, that *is* the problem being dealt with in all those passages.

Furthermore, if you do not know what the words *Arbeit Macht Frei!* mean, they mean "work will set you free." I wrote an article two or three years ago—in my opinion still one of the better ones I ever wrote—trying to help Christians. One could take that article as an attempt to explain to unbelievers how you come to Christ. It was an article written in a church bulletin specifically to Christians dealing with what I called in my paper earlier a sort of "spiritual neuroticism" that says, "Well, I would like to feel secure in my salvation, but I am not sure I have done enough." So I took the words that were over the death camps of so many Nazi places like Auschwitz and Buchenwald, "work will set you free," and said, "You know, that is something of what I have known of people doing in their Christian lives!" Maybe I am the only one who has ever met anybody like this, but people who were just spiritually insecure because they were not sure they had done enough.

My dad, on his death bed in this town said: "Rubel, I know I don't have many more days to live. I just hope that when I stand before the Lord, I've done enough." And I said: "Daddy! That any of us preachers ever taught the gospel so that somebody as decent and godly as you would lie on his deathbed and worry that he has not done enough horrifies me. No, you have *not*, Daddy. You have not done enough to go to heaven, but Jesus has done enough to get you there. This life of faith that you have lived—flawed obedience to God, still sinful—this life of faith access you have lived before God, you stand secure in that in God's grace. But not because *you* have done enough."

Lest anyone ever misunderstand again my intent in writing *Arbeit Macht Frei!*, let me say: I just accept the responsibility for being a poor communicator who did not label the article: "This is not to unbelievers about becoming Christians; this is to Christians, about living in confidence." But I do not think most of us do that sort of labeling of our writings. But if you look at the things that were talked about later in the article, they are not the things that have to do with obedience to the gospel and becoming a Christian. I affirm that as emphatically as any of these men on the stage or in the chairs in front of me. But I affirm that some of those who are in Christ, who have a covenant relationship with God, live by a "slanderous and outrageous" lie that holds we can only feel secure about our salvation if we think we have *done enough*. We have not. And we do not contribute one whit to the ground of our salvation. That is the free gift of God through Christ.

Romans, Galatians, Ephesians 2—all inveigh against anybody thinking anything other than the death of Jesus is the ground of our salvation, that out of which our confidence arises. In the Christian life, we are called to progressive sanctification, to grow in the likeness of Christ. But we will never be sanctified because we have done enough even there. But acting in good faith, confessing constantly (1 Jno. 1:9) that we are still sinful, God holds us secure in his grace. Work does *not* set us free. Understanding of the gospel—the good news that we have been redeemed by the blood of Christ and we are held secure by grace—that is what sets us free from the neuroticism that hangs up lots of folks who are in the pews of churches that you and I preach to. And I do not think they became neurotics because we were preaching the gospel as gospel. I think they became neurotics because we preached the gospel more often in the tone of guilt. I may be mistaken about that, but that is my opinion.

Hicks: I think there is a passage that would help us here in Romans 9:30-32. We have a situation where Jews had the law of God. It was a holy law, it was a just law, it was a right law, it was a good law. They had the principle of faith by which they were going to be saved. And yet they took the law and made it into something that it was not intended to be. They tried to establish their own righteousness, to contribute their own righteousness in a way that was not intended by the law

(Rom. 9:30). "But Israel who pursued a law of righteousness has not attained it." Why not? "Because they pursued it, not by faith, but as if it were by works." There is one trying to contribute righteousness to his salvation, to contribute to the ground. I had a conversation with a feeble man in bad health which deeply impressed me. He contemplated his own death, he began to tell me about his good works. He felt good about those good works. He had planted several churches; he had ministered for forty years. But then, on the other hand, he started saying, "John Mark, I ran people away from the church sometimes. I offended people; they never came back. I told them the wrong things. I taught the wrong thing sometimes. He said, "I just do not have any assurance." If Philippians 3 applies, it applies there. If we are going to boast and cry, it is through faith, and not by a recounting of our good deeds. I am afraid that sometimes we have unintentionally created a situation where our people sit in the pew wondering whether they are saved or not. They struggle with doubt and assurance because they do not know whether they have done enough.

Moderator: I think I will cut this off at this point now. I did tolerate it because I had some evidence from several groups that people found it very difficult to hear what Rubel said today because they were thinking so much about things he had written before. And if it contributes to someone's being understood accurately, whether or not you agree with him, I think that serves Christian purposes. It is always, it seems to me, counterproductive for a Christian to misrepresent someone else, or to try to function properly when you do not understand him. And I would do as much for any of our other speakers today. I hope that will clear the air somewhat; and I am not thereby saying I approve or disapprove of whatever is said. It is only to clarify a point. Now I think we will proceed with the next question, please.

Question: *Rubel, this one is for you as well. I think in some ways you probably have already addressed this. There are really two questions. Can a person live and die as a member of the Baptist Church and go to heaven? Then the second question that is similar. Suppose I have a Methodist friend who wishes to be baptized but thinks he was saved at some earlier point. Should he be baptized and, if so, will he be my brother in Christ?*

Shelly: The first question is one I am going to leave to God. I do not know if Campbell had still been in the Brush Run Baptist Church and had died with his understanding of faith and baptism whether he would have gone to heaven or hell. I just do not believe those questions are mine to answer. They may be hypothetically of great concern to one way of approaching Scripture, but my way of approaching Scripture is to leave judgment where God says he has placed it.

The second question is much easier for me to answer—whether a person is member of the Baptist Church, Methodist Church, whatever, if that person is asking me about baptism and whether he or she should be baptized or whether that should be immersion, or whether one has been sprinkled or immersed as an infant and now is thirty-seven and rethinking the subject. What am I going to do? I am going to teach what I believe the New Testament says about the nature of baptism as a faith response to the death, burial, and resurrection of Christ. I am probably going to camp around Romans 6. That is going to allow me to affirm the proper mode of baptism as burial in water, a symbol of his death, burial, resurrection. It is going to imply some things about the degree of understanding one has about the relationship between baptism and Jesus; the faith that I have is being affirmed now in baptism—that I am trusting not my good works, but I am trusting what Jesus did in his death, burial, and resurrection as the basis for my salvation. And I will encourage that person, whether his or her background has been in a denominational body, or having lived as an agnostic, or having grown up in a building with "Church of Christ" over the door, if that is *not* what he had done, if that is *not* what he understood, if that is not the gospel he received and obeyed, my encouragement to him is that he follow this teaching from the word of God so that he may have the assurance that is grounded upon that.

Mosher: I was looking out at you while Rubel was talking and I saw two groups of faces, which is very sad to me. Second Corinthians 13:5 teaches us that we can examine ourselves and know whether or not we are in the faith. How a Baptist could examine himself and find himself in the faith is a logical impossibility. If he is not in the faith, he is not in Christ. Now God said that he (God, Christ) is the savior of the body. I do not set myself up as any man's judge, but I know that when I was in the Presbyterian Church and I read Acts 8, I knew exactly what was wrong with me. I was lost. Are we going to take that message away from people? Is that what we are about, this generation? We are going to take that hope away because we are afraid to come down where God's word comes down? Are we trying to appear loving and generous to every man that walks on the face of the earth? Brothers and sisters, the loving and generous thing to do is to tell folks, "Examine yourselves. Are you in the faith?" Let them decide, but at least give them the chance to find out whether or not they are in the faith. One can know that, and then can know whether he is right with God.

Shelly: I think that is exactly what I said: that I would teach him the gospel and let him examine his own heart and relationship. The text says for him to examine himself, not for me to examine his credentials.

Campbell was not rebaptized when he left the Baptist Church to establish an independent congregation of "just Christians." I believe that he was, in fact, obedient to the gospel in a setting that he needed later to leave, and that in the progression of his understanding—what he did there [i.e., in the Baptist Church] that was correct—did not need to be redone later.

I have met any number of people who had denominational settings, have obeyed the gospel as they have examined themselves against the light of this; and it is not mine to tell him, "No you didn't, because you didn't do it in the Church of Christ and your baptism wasn't administered at the hands of one of our people." Now I do not think that is a matter of compromising the gospel. I think that is a matter of doing what Paul said. You preach the word and each examines himself. And when he tells me, "That's what I believe and that's what I did," my answer is that in his obedience to that gospel, he was made a part of the body of Christ.

"But he was in a denomination." I will quote Brother F. W. Smith who said: "I have found Christians in lots of places they should not be in and I have encouraged them to come out." Well, so do I. But not to redo anything that they learned correctly or did correctly to that point in their lives. He does not have to be retaught the virgin birth of Christ if he affirms that. He does not need to redo his baptism if he tells me, "That was my understanding and that is what I did in obedience to the gospel in that setting."

Woodson: Take the time to read the *Porter-Tingley De-*

bate. And in that debate where Glenn V. Tingley is affirming salvation by faith only before and without water baptism (W. Curtis Porter and Glenn V. Tingley, *Porter-Tingley Debate*, 1947: 180). In his explanation he says this: I teach "Christians" they "ought to be baptized." I teach them that it is a "command" of God. But—he said, that is not the "issue" between us. The issue is whether baptism is necessary "to be saved." That is a very, very important point here. Now, whether a person believes and is baptized as Jesus says is extremely important. And to say that, "he that believeth and is baptized shall be saved" is one thing. To say "he that believeth and is saved shall be baptized" is an entirely different thing. And floating in this discussion is a very crucial question and that is whether one is saved by faith before and without baptism to be saved. That is a fundamental question.

There is struggling in the womb of our brotherhood this day, two conflicting views of faith, repentance, confession, and baptism as it relates to the grace and mercy of God. And if the view prevails that the Bible teaches "he that believeth and is saved shall be baptized," then we will have a different brotherhood. I will not live to see it, I hope. I will be dead. But you will. Those of you that are young men, you will live to see that. There is a profound difference, more than just the words, between "he that believeth and is saved shall be baptized" and "he that believeth and is baptized shall be saved." And, brethren, this discussion is not confined just to me and the other participants on this panel. This is, to chance a figure, a fire burning throughout our brotherhood. And what we are discussing today is at the very tap root of what our brotherhood is about, and make no mistake about it. On the subject of how to become a child of God, when you get through with all of the discussion, the question still gets down to this: do you believe "he that believeth and is baptized shall be saved by the grace of God?" Or do you believe "he that believes and is saved by the grace of God shall be baptized"? Read the *Porter-Tingley Debate* and that will discuss the point.

Question: *This question to brother Shelly and any of the panelists. At what point is one saved?*

Shelly: One is saved when his obedience to the gospel in a living faith shows itself in repentance and baptism in the name of Jesus.

Moderator: I would be surprised if any of our panelists would deny that. Frankly, I have not heard any of them say it.

Shelly: I think at times we are a brotherhood that operates by scare tactics. Maybe I just live in a narrow world. I have never heard anyone in our fellowship teach: "He that believes is saved and then may be baptized." I have never heard that. I do not know anyone who wants to be a champion of that. I do not know of anyone in our fellowship who has written that or preached that. And I think this sort of scare tactic that says, "Look, if we talk about grace, if we talk about the fact that if we ever admit that somebody like a Campbell could in a denominational setting do what our rhetoric has always said we believe people could do, (i.e., they just come to the word and believe that and do what it says), it is going to make them Christians. If we are now so frightened of allowing that possibility, that to discuss it, to raise it, to acknowledge it, to bump into those people, and to allow them to come and stand on a non-sectarian, undenominational platform is something now that must frighten us, we are abandoning even our historical heritage and we are denying that the gospel has the power that we have preached.

So I do not know anyone, have never heard nor read of anyone in our fellowship teaching: "He that believes is saved and then can be baptized." And the scare tactic of thinking that by discussing these things we are somehow embracing or implying or opening the door to that, I really deplore.

Moderator: I think I have known a few, Rubel, but they went out from us, because they were not of us.

Question: *This question evolved in the clarification of the discussion. But as a follow-up to one of the things that has been said, how do we keep from leaving the wrong impression if we preach so heavily on the grace of God being a free gift? How do we keep, then, from leaving out the other part? How do we make sure that we have that balance in our message? I am asking anyone who would like to respond.*

Mosher: The best way I know not to leave a false impression with folks when you are preaching is not to preach. (After a pause, brother Woodson asks, "Are you done?") I must have left a false impression with brother Woodson!

Woodson: I want to comment briefly on that very point. As I prepared for this session today, I took the time to read again the *Nichols-Holder Debate*, to read the *Porter-Bogard Debate*, to read the *Hardeman-Bogard Debate*, and to read the *Woods-Nunnery Debate*. Now I know that sounds old-fashioned and old-fogey, but when you read those books carefully, you will find that the balance between grace and faith and obedience to the gospel has been our heritage. Now where the notion arose that our folk have embraced legalism, I do not know. If somebody has embraced legalism about faith, repentance, confession, and baptism, that is wrong, that is wrong. And they ought to renounce it. But if you want to learn how to preach the plan of salvation, you go back and, first of all, read the book of Acts and saturate your mind with the cases of conversion. Then you read the epistles of Paul and Peter and James that look back, as Rick tried to discuss this morning and did an effective job in doing it, and see that the Christian life draws upon the change that came in faith, repentance, confession, and baptism. You see that and preach that. And then see from the discussions that have gone on in our brotherhood with various religious bodies over our history, see how the men that have gone before have maintained this balance. Now if somebody is out there preaching legalism, they ought not to do it. But that is not our heritage as a people.

Now on the matter of someone who is not baptized by somebody in the church of Christ, I never have known of our people doing it; that is not my knowledge. I have never known of brethren refusing to receive someone into fellowship who has been baptized in obedience to the gospel of Christ, regardless of whoever immersed him. Up near Oneida, Tennessee—you will take the time and see I am telling you the truth—years ago when men from Lipscomb went up in there in tent meetings in the early 1900s, they met a group of people who for years had preached and practiced baptism for remission of sins. And those folk up there, calling themselves Baptists, said, "We believe and teach the same thing you do." And those brethren then said, "We are in fellowship with God and with one another. You need to lay aside your denominational background and we need to live and work together." When I was in Oneida a few years ago, the brethren said, "We can take you to one of those churches that was led out of that Baptist practice and is now one of the churches of Christ in this county." Some of us could give instances within the churches where we preach where a person was immersed in obedience to Jesus Christ in order to be saved by a Baptist or Presbyterian or whoever, and they have been, and as far as I know, will continue to be accepted into fellowship.

Now as to scare tactics, I have no desire to scare anybody. There is a difference between scaring people and looking at the facts as they are being presented in books and articles and speeches and tapes that are available and easily obtained. There is a difference between being alert and being scared.

Shelly: To bring in the minority report, at least with William and my experience with people, I have known a number of people that would not be accepted on their baptism precisely because it was not done by one of our people. I have known of several. [Responding to a panelist who said: "That is a mistake."] Yes, it *is* a mistake! Keith was telling me that at the Memphis School of Preaching they actually marked five men who were teaching that in an adjoining state. They marked them for teaching it as false doctrine. And God bless you, because it *is* false doctrine.

A person hears and obeys the gospel in any context, and that person's new birth in the family of God is a reality. Now where he needs to nest and be nurtured is something I want to discuss with him, but I do not want to redo his baptism. So I do know for a fact that that has happened any number of times in our fellowship.

I am convinced that the gospel has been taught as a legalism to more people than my father. I was taught it that way. I have sermon manuscripts—manuscripts, not outlines, but manuscripts—where I taught the cross is *God's* contribution and obedience to this list of commandments is *our* contribution to salvation. I believe that is false doctrine. I taught it. I learned it and I taught it; I taught it to others.

With all due respect to T. W. Brents in *Gospel Plan of Salvation*, the word *cross* appears once in that 600-page volume on the plan of salvation. *Now* when I preach the plan of salvation, I start with the love and the grace of God and the cross of Christ. But that is a different preaching pattern than I used to have. I used to use the one modeled on Brents' book. And I think our brotherhood has teethed on and used that model, and I do not believe it is the correct model. I am willing to be disagreed with, but I just choose to disagree with those of a contrary mind. And to preach it that way is to preach it as a legalism, and it is in our blood. And it is in our literature. It is in literature that I have read and written, and I know it is the perception that lots of honest and good folk—not folks looking to be captious with us—have of what they heard us saying.

Moderator: I am sure several of us have known people who would not accept such baptism. Several of you have? Yes. I think, for the most part, William is right. Our thoughtful, most scholarly brethren who have been diligent students have taken the position he has articulated.

Question: *To any panel member. Expound 2 Peter 3:18, and the question is from that: How do you grow in grace? (There is a long pause, then laughter. At last a panelist, Rick Oster, comes to the microphone.)*

Oster: I have just been trying to sit over there and learn. With all these responses we have been getting and then the exchange of ideas, this has been educational. Let me comment on a previous question. I debated whether to do this. However, now that I am up here, and given the size of the honorarium we are getting for this, I am going to do it anyway.

I did not grow up in churches of Christ and really do not have a lot of baggage that I am dealing with from the previous life that some people do apparently. I think that it is obvious as people talk about it. Nothing is wrong with that. But having grown up in a Protestant denomination where you could feel very comfortable about your security, I never really had a moment of doubt whether I was going to be saved, and my exposure to the Restoration principle was by people who preached the cross of Christ and the place of grace. And I say all that to say that I do not remember having a lot of days where I wondered whether I was going to go to heaven or if I was walking in the light. Some of these reflections that the speakers have had are from experiences that are not part of my own autobiography.

In light of that, though, I want to say, given what I see in the students at Harding Graduate School and other places, while it may never have been intended, there are people in our congregations and in our pulpits who did grow up in churches of Christ who believe they were exposed to some pretty heavy dosage of legalism. I am in no place to know where it originated or if this is some kind of mass hallucination or something in the water, but to say I have never met anyone who preached legalism, I am in no place to refute that. I can tell you there are people out there in congregations—in some of the pulpits—who believe they grew up hearing it. Now, if you have ever done counseling, you know as you hear two people arguing back and forth, a lot of people hear things that nobody else said and they misinterpret things. I think, however, it is the case that there are a lot of people out there who think they heard it growing up. And, I think that gives us then the occasion to say we do need to be careful about our speech and maybe periodically reaffirm that we are not into the business of having a legalistic religion.

Now the text in 2 Peter 3:18: "But grow in grace and knowledge of our Lord Jesus Christ. To him be the glory both now and to the day of eternity." The process of sanctification, Christian growth, is a cooperative effort in the sense that God supplies the direction. He gives us the spiritual resources. As Jesus explained in the parable of the seed and sower that for the word of God to bear fruit, it must fall on the heart, that is, a truth-seeking heart, a good heart. I think a lot of the imperatives that have to do with experiencing Christian growth have to do with our submitting to the teachings of Scripture, being taught by the grace of God—I do not think many of us really got to the Titus 2 passage which was on the program to be discussed. As you know in Titus 2, it does talk about the pedagogical function of grace, that grace teaches us these things. It has to do, I think, that this idea of growing, with letting God's word and his Spirit work in our lives to allow that to happen. I do not think it is a kind of cryptic way to say we are really in charge of our own sanctification—or something like that. I do not know if that is what was behind the question. But I think it means to allow God to grow in us, spiritual maturity. As Paul says in 1 Corinthians, one can plant and one can water. It is very clear that growth in spiritual matters can only come from God.

Woodson: Discuss Acts 20:32 in that light.

Oster: Okay. Acts 20:32. We are now taking questions from the platform. This will require an increase in my honorarium. Yes, this is a great verse. I was hoping it was this one. Acts 20:32, Paul's address to the Ephesian elders at Miletus: "And now I commend you to God and to the word of his grace which is able to build you up and to give you the inheritance among those who are sanctified." Yes, this would be pretty much the same idea of this pedagogical and edifying work of the word of God's grace. My main point would be: all the things that we need for our own godliness and life in Christ, God supplies. He is the author. He is the source. There is not another foundation except one and that is Christ Jesus. It is God who provides all these things for our spiritual growth and development.

Moderator: Does any other group leader have one question? All right Bill, one more question and that will be all.

Question: *This question is, what must we do to continue in the grace of God? It is mentioned in Acts 13:43 that Paul and Barnabas encouraged the church at Antioch of Pisidia to continue in the grace of God. Some other verses were mentioned along these lines: you can turn the grace of God into lasciviousness, Romans 6:1 misusing the grace of God, and so forth. And along with that, we went from asking how obedient do we have to be or how many good works we have to do, to how submissive do we have to be to get to heaven? And that came in along with that question of how do we continue in the grace of God enough eventually to make it? Anyone who wants to may respond to that one.*

Hicks: I think the danger is the two extremes which I pointed out in my paper. One would be an antinomian that says to continue in the grace of God is to continue with simply a disposition of trust that severs any kind of good works from our lives so that we turn the grace of God into a license for sin. That certainly would be antinomianism in its extreme, and Jude was opposing a group of people who were antinomian in that regard. On the other extreme, legalism says that we have to do twenty percent, forty percent, eighty percent, a hundred percent, or whatever it is to continue in the grace of God. The problem with that is we are all uncertain as to exactly what our percentage is. We are ignorant about a lot of things anyway. We do not know what percentage our ignorance has to do with the totality. So there are a lot of things that are involved. But I would argue that the principle of submissive faith and the willingness intentioned to submit to God and to obey God as his will is made known to us, is the principle on which we can boast in Christ and not in our good deeds throughout our life.

Mosher: I keep hearing about twenty percent and thirty percent and forty percent and that concerns me a little bit. Brother Hicks, I want to give you this dime if you will walk up here and get it, please. (Can I keep it?) Yes sir! (All right.) How much did he contribute to getting that dime? One hundred percent. He contributed himself. That is Matthew 16:24. If we are going to keep arguing over percentages, we are going to forget what the text says. It says submit yourself, contribute yourself. See, that is all I can do.

Hicks: I get a dime's worth on that. I contributed something in the sense that I received what he was willing to give. But I did not contribute anything to the ten cents he gave me. He gave me the whole dime. I did not give any part of it. This is the point. My contribution is that I am willing to go and receive it. I am willing to receive it, trusting that you are really going to give it to me. But does that mean that now I get to keep it? He says okay you can keep it as long as you do a whole list of other things and are perfect for the next twenty years, you can keep that dime. No! The point of the percentage is that we do not have to be perfect for twenty years to keep the dime. All we need to do is to continue to trust that God's gift is a gift that he continually gives to us as we continually embrace it through submissive faith.

Woodson: One verse of Scripture. I have been interested in how many verses are exegeted today. In Hebrews 10:36: "For you have need of patience that after ye have done the will of God, you might receive the promise." Greek students, aorist participle here. Mark 16, "He that believeth and is baptized"—future tense, "may obtain." We are to do the will of God as long as we live. Wherein we fail we are to recognize it, admit it to God, and say: "God, I will do my best from now on. I am sorry I failed." It is not a matter of a percentage. It is a resolve from the heart to do all I know that is God's will as long as I live. And the text says after that we shall receive the promise.

Moderator: We feel very deeply about grace and faith. We do not want to take God for granted and be irresponsible. We do not want to take into our own hands things that do not belong there. And that means that the five speakers have come at some risk to themselves and I think it would be appropriate for you to show some kind of righteous appreciation for their willingness to come and not only give their presentations but, as it were, to bare their chests to your questions, maybe barbs and so forth. But I personally am indebted to them for what they have done today, and I hope you are, too.